# LIVING IN
# NEW ENGLAND

# LIVING IN NEW ENGLAND

PHOTOGRAPHY BY
**SØLVI DOS SANTOS**
TEXT BY
**ELAINE LOUIE**

SIMON & SCHUSTER
NEW YORK · LONDON · TORONTO · SYDNEY · SINGAPORE

# CONTENTS

"The best way to learn about designing is to see how people actually live." I said this once about my own work, but it is just as applicable to interior design and especially to the beautiful homes featured in this book. The New Englanders lived simply; their houses are based on simplicity and frugality, and these traits lend themselves to a contemporary way of living. This style is one I feel close to – its simplicity and timelessness reflect my own feelings about fashion design and I have always believed in the critical link that connects fashion and lifestyle.

From the first minute I saw my house in Connecticut, I knew I loved it. Its spare simplicity spoke directly to my own convictions about design. My work is all about reduction, stripping down the design to its pure essentials, and the same is true of my eighteenth-century stone tavern and its décor. I've kept the spaces relatively plain, with a clarity that reflects

# FOREWORD by BILL BLASS

OPPOSITE FASHION DESIGNER BILL BLASS BOUGHT THIS HOUSE, SITUATED IN 22 ACRES OF LAND IN NEW PRESTON, CONNECTICUT, IN 1976. WHEN IT WAS BUILT IN 1770, ITS ORIGINAL FUNCTION WAS A TAVERN, WHICH WAS ONCE HONORED BY A VISIT BY GEORGE WASHINGTON.

RIGHT BLASS CALLS THIS STATUE "THE ALLEGORICAL DOG"; ITS PROVENANCE IS UNKNOWN, ALTHOUGH IT IS PROBABLY ENGLISH OR CONTINENTAL. A LIVELY, ALMOST ANIMATED CANINE, BLASS BELIEVES THAT IT IS BAYING AT THE MOON.

the region's historical style. In this context, a blank wall can feel like a luxury. This simplicity is not only the essence of the Puritan tradition of New England but also a very contemporary attitude toward living. As much as I love my house, it's not meant to impress – this is a place in which I can be quite comfortable living rather than an architectural monument.

This is something Sølvi dos Santos understood when she photographed my house, and simplicity in every respect became the theme of her visit – together with her sensitive attitude, full of perception and observation. It's an idea that plays a major role throughout this book. As a photographer, Sølvi sees clearly and cleanly to the essence of a house. The day she came to Connecticut, she entered into the soul of the house and garden. The resulting photographs show the closeness that she achieves with her subject. I don't believe in the notions of good or bad taste – it is all in the eye of the beholder – and Sølvi sees with the eyes of a true artist. The detail of her photographs is reflected in Elaine Louie's interviews, and together they provide us with a fascinating view of 25 of the most inspirational and stylish homes in New England.

Bill Blass
New Preston, Connecticut

7

When explorer Captain John Smith received a royal charter from the Virginia Company of London, he sailed from England to the Chesapeake Bay and, in 1607, founded the first permanent English settlement in North America at Jamestown, Virginia. Seven years later, on another expedition, Captain Smith mapped the coast from Penobscot Bay to Cape Cod, and gave those six states, Maine, Vermont, New Hampshire, Massachusetts, Rhode Island and Connecticut, the name of New England. Most of the original seventeenth-century settlers were English, many of them Calvinists or Puritans, who believed in plain and religious living. Some of the early homes, especially in northern New England, were farms, continuous buildings where each part had its own function – the main house, a barn for the cows or sheep, and a shed for chickens and pigs. But many of the settlers had brought with them the

# INTRODUCTION

OPPOSITE THE ARTIST JAMIE WYETH AND HIS WIFE, PHYLLIS, SPEND PART OF THE YEAR ON SOUTHERN ISLAND, MAINE. THE MAIN HOUSE, BUILT IN THE NINETEENTH CENTURY, AND THE LIGHTHOUSE NEARBY FACE SOUTH AT THE MOUTH OF THE PENOBSCOT BAY, STANDING OUT BRILLIANTLY AGAINST THE WATER, SKY AND GRASS.

RIGHT THE OCEAN NOT ONLY DOMINATES THE LANDSCAPE, IT HAS ALSO INSPIRED THE DECORATION OF THE WYETHS' HOME. EVEN ITS CAST-OFFS ARE TREASURED – HERE A BUCKET OF SAND DOLLARS, COLLECTED OVER THE YEARS, SITS BY A DOOR

culture and the architecture of England. The earliest seventeenth-century homes were one-room wood houses. Then a shed was added, a center chimney, and a second story. As people prospered, they began to emulate the more elaborate styles that were popular in England. By the eighteenth century, some homeowners, like merchants or shipowners, started building Georgian houses with square layout, central hallway, and doorway framed by columns supporting a pediment. In the nineteenth century, the Georgian house was transformed into a more refined Federal style that included larger window openings and more slender muntins. The door became wider and taller and was topped by a fanlight and flanked by sidelights. From 1820 to 1860, the Greek Revival style held sway, with facades designed as two-story temple fronts with pedimented gables. The second half of the nineteenth century saw the emergence of the Victorian style, with fanciful gingerbread trim, turrets, exploded bay windows and gas lights. Plate glass encouraged bigger windows. By the twentieth century, the mill towns that had dotted New England declined as industry went south, and New England had to reinvent itself again. High-technology businesses surround Boston. Hartford, Connecticut, calls itself the insurance capital of the country, while Nantucket and Martha's Vineyard are sleepy in winter and tourist havens in the summer.

*Living in New England* is an album of 25 different houses that shows how the owners embrace not only the New England architecture, but also the land, the vistas, and the seasons. Within New England, each of the six

**RIGHT** IN THE WYETHS' HOMES,
FURNITURE HAS BEEN CHOSEN TO BLEND IN
WITH THIS NINETEENTH CENTURY HOUSE.
IN THE MAIN HOUSE, THE WHOLE OF THE
FIRST FLOOR IS A HUGE SPACE
THAT INCLUDES THE LIVING ROOM, DINING
ROOM, BEDROOM, BUT IS MAINLY USED AS A
STUDIO, EACH AREA DEFINED SOLELY BY A
FEW PIECES OF FURNITURE.
A SOFA COVERED IN BLUE-STRIPED BEIGE
LINEN MARKS THIS PART OF
THE ROOM AS THE LIVING AREA.
THE PAINTING OF A "BRIG IN ROUGH SEA"
BY THOMAS BIRCH (1779–1851)
IS THE ONLY OBJECT IN THE
ROOM SUGGESTING ANYTHING OTHER
THAN TRANQUILITY AND ORDER.
IN BOTH THE HOMES ON SOUTHERN
ISLAND, EVERYTHING, WHETHER
A CUPBOARD, A BOOK, OR A STOOL,
LOOKS LIKE IT HAS BEEN TOUCHED BY
GENERATIONS OF PEOPLE,
SO THAT EVEN WHEN NO ONE IS HOME,
THE ROOMS FEEL LIVED-IN.

states has its own personality. Connecticut, whose original inhabitants were the Algonquin, has beaches and harbors, rolling hills and lakes. The landscape is gentle. When you are in northwest Connecticut, it is so quiet it feels like you can hear a leaf drop. The Connecticut houses in this book possess a kind of genteelness that matches the landscape.

But if Connecticut is genteel, Maine is rugged. Like Norway, the state has more trees than people. It is 80 percent forest and has a wild, rocky coast. When you drive the highway or roads in Maine, it is sometimes so desolate of people that for miles and miles the only view is of trees, lit softly by the low-lying sun. The people of Maine are a mix of English, Irish and Scottish, some French, a few Indians and African Americans, all known for their taciturn, dry humor. Shipbuilding was once an important trade, and those same skills survive, often translated into the building of homes rather than boats. Floors don't creak. Walls are plumb. Houses have a deep solidity about them. The homes range from a farm to Federal, Greek Revival, Gothic and Victorian.

Two American presidents, John Quincy Adams and John F. Kennedy have lived in the Commonwealth of Massachusetts, as the state is known. Other famous literary inhabitants include Edith Wharton, Eugene O'Neill, and Norman Mailer. The Boston Tea Party helped trigger the Revolutionary War and Boston is now fêted as the birthplace of American independence and the region is still steeped in national pride.

The earliest settlers arrived in New Hampshire in 1623 to fish and trade, and in 1629, the region was named after the English county of Hampshire. Although it is heavily forested and rural, more than one-third of its residents now work in manufacturing. Every four years, however, New Hampshire has its 15 minutes of frenzied, national fame when it is the first state to hold a Presidential primary election.

Rhode Island is the smallest state in America, founded in 1636 by Roger Williams as a refuge for religious dissenters; but by the end of the nineteenth century, the very rich were coming to spend their summers in Newport to play, dance, and sail.

The French were the first settlers in Vermont – the name derives from the French words *verte* (green) and *monte* (mountain). A few American colonial customs are still upheld here – voters take a "freeman's oath" to be "of a quiet and peaceable behavior."

But the common theme behind all these states is their love of nature and the four seasons, a passion that is reflected in the New England homes featured in this book.

in the COUNTRY

Chase Hill Farm lies near the coast in Ashaway, Rhode Island, and is the home of award-winning designer, Stephen Mack. Set on 50 acres of rolling fields, mixed woodland, streams and ponds, it neatly defines his work. With cows in the distance and sheep grazing lazily nearby, it is authentic, if not quintessential, New England and this bucolic atmosphere pervades every corner of this environment.

Built in 1792, the eighteenth-century architecture of Chase Hill Farm and its environs are, in Mack's own words, "a study in subtlety, the elegance of simplicity". He creates homes and estates along these lines – be they formal or rustic, the characteristics of subtlety and simplicity run through his work. Mack has collected and continues to collect endangered and remarkable houses, barns and outbuildings – all that is necessary to produce and restore estates with atmosphere.

# RESTORED IDYLL

OPPOSITE WITH THE WIDE DUTCH DOOR SWUNG OPEN, MACK HAS PULLED A SMALL TAVERN TABLE IN FRONT OF THE DOORWAY FOR A VIEW OF THE MEADOW. HE REMOVED THE MODERN PLASTER FROM THE OAK WALLS, GLUING LINEN STRIPS OVER THE EDGES AND THE KNOT HOLES TO PRESERVE THE ROOM'S ORIGINAL FINISH. FOR THE SAME REASON, HE HAS CHOSEN TO LIGHT THIS ROOM SOLELY BY CANDLES; IN FACT, IN THE TWENTY YEARS MACK HAS LIVED HERE, HE HAS NEVER USED AN ELECTRICAL LIGHT IN THIS ROOM.

RIGHT LIGHT PASSES THROUGH THE SWIRLED EIGHTEENTH-CENTURY GLASS AND CLIMBS UP THE DOOR IN THE MORE FORMAL PARLOR.

He maintains a stock of 25 to 30 meticulously disassembled structures which he then entwines with the design of his new projects. These reconstructed buildings combined with the new design result in a seamless joining of the eighteenth and twenty-first centuries. As Mack says, "they are places where you can breathe".

Following the traditions of architecture in New England, the material of choice has always been wood. Chase Hill Farm has a hand-hewn oak framework, with wide oak floors, wood clapboards and a wood shingle roof. Other structures, such as barns, outbuildings, and studio, are also entirely built of wood.

Over the course of the years, during the course of his work, Mack has amassed a vast knowledge of design history as well as some wonderful furniture and other objects that he now displays in his own home. He firmly believes that the interior, as well as the exterior of the house, should reflect as faithfully as possible, the history of the house.

Inside the house, the plaster is whitewashed and a warm off-white. The woodwork is painted in subdued colors of milk paint, and the floors are unfinished and scrubbed. The walls of the kitchen are oak planks which were typical for the period and Mack has covered their joints with linen and cotton, whitewashed to look like plaster. The colors, textures, and furnishings melt together in the late afternoon light. It is this bringing of the house to its essentials that appeals to Mack. Truly, this house is the epitome of his 'elegant simplicity'.

**LEFT** RED MILK PAINT, NOT DISSIMILAR
TO THE COLOR OF THE HOUSE,
CREATES A WARM STAIR HALL JUST
INSIDE THE FRONT DOOR.
THE OVAL PAINTING OF A SCOTTISH BOY
WITH HIS DOG AND AN
EIGHTEENTH-CENTURY CANDLESTICK
PLACED ON A BRASS-TOP TABLE
RESCUED FROM THE YALE CLUB
ADD INTEREST TO AN OFT-FORGOTTEN AREA.
ANCIENT HORSE TACK HANG
OVER THE BANNISTER.

**RIGHT** MACK'S FRIENDS HAVE TO
STEP ONTO THE CHEST TO
CLIMB INTO THIS UNUSUALLY HIGH
1830S FOUR-POSTER BED
IN THE GUEST BEDROOM UNDER
THE EAVES. "SOME OF MY
OLDER GUESTS ASKED
IF I'D MAKE BED STAIRS FOR THEM"
HE SAYS. THE QUILT DATES
FROM THE MID-NINETEENTH CENTURY.

**OPPOSITE** THE GRANITE SINK IS HAND CARVED AND IS OLDER THAN THE HOUSE ITSELF, ALTHOUGH THE BRASS FAUCETS DATE FROM THE EARLY TWENTIETH CENTURY. MACK POLISHES THEM ONCE A WEEK. HE DOES ALL THE WASHING UP HERE — ALTHOUGH THE HOUSE HAS CENTRAL HEATING, ELECTRICITY, AND OTHER MODERN-DAY AMENITIES, MACK IS THE DISHWASHER, AND HAPPILY SO, HE SAYS. IN THE GRANITE SOAP DISH SITS A MEMENTO OF HIS YOUTH, A FRESH BAR OF OLD-FASHIONED FELS-NAPTHA LAUNDRY SOAP. "IT SMELLS GOOD," SAYS MACK. "MY MOTHER USED TO WASH ME WITH IT WHEN I ENCOUNTERED POISON IVY."

**RIGHT** MACK'S KITCHEN DESIGN CENTERS AROUND SIMPLE CABINETS AND OPEN SHELVES. THE COUNTERTOP IS CHESNUT, PEPPERED WITH "DUTCHMEN", SMALL INLAYS TO HEAL THE WOUNDS OF 200 YEARS. A COLLECTION OF LUSTERWARE CUPS AND SAUCERS, CHINESE EXPORT PORCELAIN, CROCKS, AND ALL MANNER OF OTHER EARLY KITCHEN ACCOUTREMENTS IS DISPLAYED ON OPEN SHELVES. MACK POINTS OUT "EVERYTHING GETS USED, IT'S NOT JUST FOR LOOK,". HE PAUSES AND SAYS, "THAT'S THE FUN OF IT."

One day in 1976, Billy Baldwin, the late interior designer, took his friend Bill Blass to see a tavern that had been built in 1770, nestling among 22 acres of land in Connecticut. Blass saw it, bought it, and has since turned the house into an airy home where sun pours into every room. New England homes, he says, are based on simplicity and frugality, and these qualities lend themselves to a contemporary attitude of sparseness and absence of clutter, which has created the perfect retreat from the bustle of New York. Blass is one of the most prominent of America's fashion designers, who has created elegant clothes for real people. He has created a look that is completely nonchalant – such as throwing a camel hair polo coat over an elegant evening dress or pairing a cashmere sweater with a silk taffeta skirt. Blass is also a philanthropist who has given $10 million to the New York Public Library.

# ART AND DESIGN

OPPOSITE BLASS HATES CLUTTER, AND THE FRONT HALL OF HIS EIGHTEENTH-CENTURY HOUSE IS ARRANGED TO APPEAR WARM AND INVITING WITHOUT BEING OVERFURNISHED. THE PLANT INJECTS A SHOT OF COLOR TO A NEUTRAL AREA, AND THE DOOR STOP – THE LEG OF AN OLD WOODEN STATUE – PROVIDES A TOUCH OF HUMOR.

RIGHT BLASS'S SENSE OF WIT EXTENDS TO THE GARDEN, WHERE HE HAS GROUPED TOGETHER THESE EIGHTEENTH-CENTURY STATUES AS IF THEY ARE CHATTING. IN SUCH A TIMELESSLY BEAUTIFUL SETTING, THE STATUES, WHICH HE FOUND IN LONDON AND PLACED UNDER A VAST MAPLE TREE, SEEM TO MOLD THEMSELVES TO THE SCENERY.

Blass once said that his designs epitomized purification and reduction. What he has done in his home is create airy rooms that have strong, bold pieces of furniture arranged so that they stand out against the bright white walls and white-painted floors. These striking juxtapositions also form an ideal setting for his collections of off-beat ephemera. The most inviting of the rooms is the master bedroom. The walls are painted tobacco brown, and he has covered the bed with a brown and white quilt. The drama of the room, however, comes not just from these rich colors but also from his collection of curios. There's a figure of George Washington by Jean-Antoine Houdon, an eighteenth-century French sculptor. And jutting out from the top of a chest is a model staircase, one of many architects' models that he has collected over the years. "Architects made them in order to gain membership of a guild," Blass says. What is disconcerting about this staircase is that the stairs do not lead anywhere; they twist and climb before ending abruptly in mid air.

All but one of the fireplaces in the house work. But Blass has made the non-functioning one a visual focal point. The entire fireplace is painted white, and he has transformed the corner in which it stands into a gallery of his mirror collection from England, France, Sweden, and the United States. A rectangular one with a carved eagle hangs directly over the mantel. The others – round, oval, square – are arranged on an adjacent wall. What is literally a dead spot – a non-working fireplace – is given life, with light glinting off the mirrors.

**RIGHT** MOST OF THE ROOMS IN THIS AIRY HOUSE ARE PAINTED WHITE FROM FLOOR TO CEILING. "IT LETS THE FURNITURE STAND OUT," BLASS EXPLAINS. NATURAL LIGHT POURS THROUGH THE SEVEN WINDOWS IN THE LIVING ROOM — BLASS HAS MADE SURE THAT NONE OF THE FURNITURE IS HIGHER THAN THE WINDOW SILL SO THAT THE LIGHT CAN ENTER WITHOUT OBSTRUCTION. INSTEAD OF THE CONVENTIONAL COFFEE TABLE, EASY CHAIRS AND SOFA, BLASS HAS USED MORE DRAMATIC FURNITURE — A GAMING TABLE CENTERS THE ROOM WHILE A PAIR OF GLOBES FLANK THE NINETEENTH-CENTURY ENGLISH BOOKCASE. IT CALLS TO MIND THE ORIGINAL PURPOSE OF THE SPACE AS A GENTLEMEN'S WAITING ROOM. THE ELEGANT BALANCE OF THE PICTURES ON THE FAR WALL ADDS TO AN OVERALL IMPRESSION OF CALM, ORDERLY COMFORT.

**LEFT** A BLACK PAINTED FLOOR ADDS AN URBAN TOUCH TO A WHITE GUEST BEDROOM. BLASS RAISED THE MINIATURE WOOD HOUSE, WHICH WAS PROBABLY ORIGINALLY A GIFT BOX, SO IT COULD BE USED AS A NIGHTSTAND. ABOVE IT HANGS AN ARCHITECTURAL WATERCOLOR OF ANOTHER COLUMNED BUILDING.

**LEFT BELOW** THIS ROOM, JUST OFF THE HALLWAY, WAS PAINTED IN VARIOUS SHADES OF GRAY, AND FURNISHED WITH A NINETEENTHTH-CENTURY ENGLISH HALL CHAIR AND A ROUND TABLE, WHICH BLASS THINKS ARE "PROBABLY SWEDISH PORPHYRY."

**RIGHT** IN THE MASTER BEDROOM, THE WALLS ARE PAINTED A WARM TOBACCO BROWN, WITH THE CEILINGS AND TRIM A BRIGHT WHITE SO THAT LIGHT COMING THROUGH THE WINDOW REFLECTS ON THE SILLS AND BOUNCES OFF THE CEILING. THE COLOR SCHEME OF THE WALLS IS ECHOED IN THE COLORS OF THE QUILT, AND THE ZIGZAG OF THE QUILT PATTERN IS ECHOED IN THE SILHOUETTE OF THE ARCHITECTURAL MODEL OF A STAIRCASE THAT GOES NOWHERE. BLASS SUSPECTS THAT THE STAIRCASE IS ENGLISH, AND THAT ARCHITECTS MADE THEM IN ORDER TO PROVE THAT THEY WERE SKILLFUL ENOUGH TO JOIN A GUILD. A BUST OF GEORGE WASHINGTON BY AN EIGHTEENTH-CENTURY FRENCH SCULPTOR PLACED NEXT TO THE BED COMMEMORATES WASHINGTON'S MEETING HERE WITH A FRENCH GENERAL.

FAR LEFT ABOVE  WOOD ON WOOD:
IN THE DINING ROOM, A CARVED WOODEN
BUST OF A NINETEENTH-CENTURY
ADMIRAL, ONCE A SHIP'S FIGUREHEAD, SITS
ALERT, THOUGH SLIGHTLY WORN, ON A
PLAIN, STURDY MAPLE TABLE.

FAR LEFT BELOW  BLASS IS A COMPULSIVE
COLLECTOR, AND IN THIS TINY WHITE ROOM
IS A GROUP OF IDIOSYNCRATIC MIRRORS.
THEY ARE A STUDY OF FRAME STYLES FROM
FRANCE, ENGLAND, SWEDEN, AND THE
UNITED STATES. THE WHITE PITCHER GIVES A
FOCUS TO THE ONLY FIREPLACE IN THE
HOUSE THAT DOESN'T WORK.

LEFT  "I DIDN'T SHOOT THIS," EXPLAINS
BLASS OF THE SPECTACULAR ANTLERS THAT
ONCE BELONGED TO A SMALL DEER AND
NOW HANG IN THE DINING ROOM.

RIGHT  EVEN THE MUD ROOM, THE
HOMELIEST ROOM IN THE HOUSE,
IS INTRIGUING. THE TWIG BENCH, LIKE ALL
TWIG FURNITURE, IS A GENRE NOTED FOR ITS
IDIOSYNCRASY BUT NOT FOR ITS COMFORT.
BUT THEN HOW LONG DOES IT TAKE TO
REMOVE A PAIR OF SNOWBOOTS? SO TOO THE
ANTLER COAT RACK. IT'S NOT A PLACE TO
HANG CHIFFON, BUT IT CAN EASILY TAKE A
FEW STRAWHATS AND RAIN JACKETS.

In New England, there is an old tradition of buying houses and then moving them from one site to another (which is apparently no different from moving logs from one place to another, and is actually cheaper than building a new house from scratch). When landscape artist Neil Welliver's house in Lincolnville, Maine, was destroyed in a fire in 1975, he and his late wife, Polly Mudge, found a sagging boat building two miles up the road. He bought, dismantled and moved the 16,000 square-foot construction, marking every stick of wood, numbering each piece of timber and hiring 12 people to reassemble and strengthen the house.

This painstaking reconstruction has left him as familiar with every beam and rafter in his 1800s house as he is with the beaver houses, osprey nests, and burnt forests that fill his paintings. He casually observes, as easily as he might comment on the weather, the original intentions of every

# LABOR OF LOVE

piece of furniture, from table to fireplace. He recites a litany of his furnishings, an eclectic mix of eighteenth-, nineteenth-, and twentieth-century pieces, with the joy that comes from knowing how they were built, coming as he does from a long line of cabinetmakers. Each room is capacious and each piece of furniture has a boldness of scale combined with a generous sense of comfort. You can sprawl, spread out, curl up and read. Throughout the house are apothecary chests – big, plain wood cupboards usually left in the original color, whether a gray-green or a mustard gray-green. "I never, never take the color off," Welliver says. "It reduces the value by 75 percent." In each room, there is a shot of color. In the kitchen, it's the yellow ice cream parlor chairs dating from the Twenties. On the porch, it's a sea green chair and a moss green door, although both bursts of color compete for attention with the moose head.

Welliver grew up in northern Pennsylvania in an area that was once totally wild and untamed. In Maine, he has amassed 2,500 acres of land, most of which he has donated to the Coastal Mountain Land Trust. His property is a sanctuary for moose and deer, bear, and wild turkey. He claims he has even seen a moose fall in love with a cow. Each day he paints, either outdoors, where the wildflowers grow among the sunflowers, lilies and hollyhocks, or in his studio, where he works on square canvases, painting from top to bottom until he is finished. For Welliver, who is happiest close to nature, living in the northernmost part of New England is not a matter of style, or even choice. He belongs there.

LEFT WELLIVER KEEPS FIRES BURNING THROUGHOUT HIS HOUSE YEAR-ROUND. A NINETEENTH-CENTURY RUMFORD FIREPLACE, BUILT WIDE AND SHALLOW SO THAT THE HEAT FLOWS OUT INTO THE ROOM, WARMS THE LIVING ROOM. ALTHOUGH THE FURNITURE IS FROM DIFFERENT PERIODS, WHETHER EIGHTEENTH-, NINETEENTH-, OR TWENTIETH-CENTURY, IT IS ALL LINKED BY ITS STRONG, CLEAN LINES. THE COWSKIN RUG PROVIDES A BOLD, GRAPHIC FLOOR COVERING, COUNTERING THE UNDERSTATED LOOK OF THE REST OF THE ROOM.

RIGHT WELLIVER HAS A SINGULAR WAY OF PAINTING. FIRST, HE WALKS OR DRIVES IN THE 2,500 ACRES OF LAND THAT HE CALLS HOME. THEN HE CHOOSES AN IMAGE TO SKETCH, PERHAPS A GROVE OF BIRCH, A THICK, MURKY BOG, OR THE WHITENESS OF SNOW UPON TREES. HE MAKES THE SKETCH OUTSIDE, AND THEN IN THE STUDIO BEGINS THE PAINTING ITSELF.

**LEFT** IN THE KITCHEN, AN IRONING TABLE BECOMES A DINING TABLE WITH NICELY ROUNDED EDGES. THE DINING CHAIRS ARE 1920S ICE CREAM PARLOR CHAIRS. THE STOVE IS AN EAGLE NINETEENTH-CENTURY MODEL, AND OCCASIONALLY GETS USED.

**BELOW** WELLIVER CLAIMS TO BE DESCENDED FROM GENERATIONS OF CABINETMAKERS. HE IS AN ADEPT WOODWORKER, AND WHEN HIS LATE WIFE POLLY MUDGE SAW A WOODEN DISHRACK AT A CHURCH DINNER, HE MADE ONE FOR HER.

**RIGHT** WELLIVER'S PRINCIPLES OF RESTORATION AND RENOVATION EXTEND TO RECYCLING ALL UNNECESSARY OBJECTS. WITH AN ORDERLY PRECISION LEARNT FROM HIS ARTISAN ANCESTORS, HE STORES 7,000 FEET OF PINE FLOORING, ALL OLD WIDE FLOORBOARDS, IN HIS CELLAR, AND CAREFULLY SEPARATES HIS GARBAGE INTO ORGANIC AND NON-DISPOSABLE WASTE.

**ABOVE** THE HOUSE MIRRORS THE PSYCHE OF MAINE, WHICH WELLIVER DESCRIBES AS A PLACE WHERE PEOPLE ARE WITHOUT AFFECTATION. "THEY TAKE YOU AS YOU COME," HE SAYS. THE DESIGN OF THE KITCHEN EXUDES THIS FRANK UNSELFCONSCIOUSNESS – EVERYTHING IS IN THE OPEN, UNPRETENTIOUS AND TRUSTWORTHY, ARRANGED FOR COMFORT, CONVENIENCE AND EFFICIENCY RATHER THAN DISPLAY.

**ABOVE** ABOVE THE FIREPLACE, A PORTRAIT
OF WELLIVER STAKES A TERRITORIAL
CLAIM ON THE ROOM.
THE ENORMOUS BUCKET TO THE RIGHT
OF THE FIREPLACE WILL BE FILLED
WITH A BATCH OF FIREWOOD.

**RIGHT** THE BEDROOM IS A STUDY OF MUTED
COLORS AND STRONG LINEAR SHAPES.
THE RUST- AND CREAM-COLORED
QUILT, WITH ITS SHARP
BLOCK PATTERN, STANDS OUT AGAINST
THE MUTED YELLOW OF THE DOORS.
IN THIS SPARSELY FURNISHED
ROOM, EVERYTHING APPEARS TO BE A
LITTLE HIGHER THAN EXPECTED.
THE BED IS RAISED, MAKING IT FEEL
UNFUSSILY CEREMONIAL AND
AFFORDING A BETTER VIEW THROUGH
THE WINDOWS. THE PEGGED DRAWERS
REACH RIGHT TO THE
CEILING, AND THE GRAY-BLUE CABINET
ON THE RIGHT STANDS TALL.

**BELOW** THE AUSTERITY OF
THE BEDROOM IS MADE WARM BY
THE APPEALING COLORS.
WELLIVER HAS A CANNY
KNOWLEDGE OF
THE ANTIQUES MARKET
AND, LIKE ALL HIS ANTIQUE FURNITURE,
THE BROWN-BLACK CUPBOARD
RETAINS ITS ORIGINAL PAINT. "I
NEVER, NEVER TAKE THE COLOR OFF,"
SAYS WELLIVER. THE FRESHLY
PAINTED WINDOW FRAMES PROVIDE
A DASH OF COLOR.

Richard Kazarian bought his 1848 Greek Revival house in Warren, Rhode Island, in 1998 and has created within it a shrine to the humble, utilitarian, yet sculptural object. He is steeped in history – he is a holder of a Ph.D in American history and an antique seller – and this has inspired him to seek out antiques that time has often passed by. Delighting in discovering forgotten objects made by an anonymous artisan, or even a factory worker, Kazarian was one of the first to rediscover garden objects and bring garden benches, urns, pediments, and cornices from the outdoors into the home in the 1970s. "When you approach collecting from the bottom up, as opposed to the top down," he muses, "that leads to the discovery of objects that have been missing from a conventional view of antiques. You widen the periphery. It's not just folk art and itinerant artists. It's the objects that come out of factories, like a steel desk, an object whose

# PRACTICAL ART

**OPPOSITE** IN THE KITCHEN KAZARIAN HAS
CREATED A DISPLAY OF OBJECTS
UNITED BY THE CAREFUL CRAFTSMANSHIP
OF THEIR OPENWORK. A NINETEENTH-
CENTURY MASONIC WOOD KEYSTONE,
PLACED IN FRONT OF A CROSS-HATCHED
IRON GRATE, SITS ON A NINETEENTH-
CENTURY DUTCH COUNTER. TO THE LEFT
A CLAM BASKET SITS ON A STOOL, WHILE ON
THE CENTER TABLE A GOTHIC-STYLE
TOLE LIGHT FIXTURE HAS BEEN TURNED
UPSIDE DOWN TO INJECT A LITTLE HUMOR.

**RIGHT** THE PROVENANCE OF THESE ANTIQUE
PAWS IS UNKNOWN –
ALL KAZARIAN KNOWS IS THAT THEY WERE
PROBABLY BASES FROM MARBLE TUBS.

origin was far more utilitarian." He likes to see the influences of one century to another, of a modern chair that suggests the maker studied a Queen Anne chair. He accepts the fact that he may never know who the artisan was, nor the original intention of, say, a piece of wire grid. But he likes the buying, selling, and, especially, the thinking about the history.

Uniting unrelated objects by material, by architectural line, or by kind, Kazarian has arranged the collections in his house like installation art – isolated objects, mostly ornamental architectural fragments that captivate the eye, seen as objects of study rather than decoration. He points to a nineteenth-century tin rainspout painted dark orange and decorated with a graceful, delicately flowing swag. "I like to elevate the status of objects which have been ignored or undervalued," he remarks. Kazarian is an admirer of those objects executed by anonymous people. These artisans nevertheless had that gift of adding aesthetic quality to the utilitarian and so Kazarian wants people to see the rainspout as a piece of sculpture. In a second-floor bedroom, he has hung over the bed a tin panel decorated with a swag. Like the swagged rainspout, the panel, which he suspects once decorated the exterior of a building, is another plain material made fanciful by an artisan's whim. He is similarly intrigued by his nineteenth-century Dutch cabinet, or what he calls a "bank" of drawers imported by the mercantile class from Holland. For him, using primitive materials and the simplest of forms to achieve the height of sophistication is akin to the artistic skill involved in the creation of a Louis Seize commode.

**LEFT ABOVE**  IN A SECOND-FLOOR BEDROOM, KAZARIAN HAS CREATED A SMALL STILL LIFE, JUXTAPOSING A NINETEENTH-CENTURY FRENCH BAROMETER AND A COLLECTION OF TIN HANDS.

**LEFT BELOW**  IN A CORRIDOR LEADING TOWARDS THE LOUVERED FRONT DOOR STANDS AN EIGHTEENTH-CENTURY ITALIAN CISTERN CLAD IN LEAD, WHICH ONCE CARRIED WATER OR WINE. ITS IDIOSYNCRASY IS ITS BEAUTIFULLY DETAILED ARTISANSHIP. "THE TOP FINIAL AND AROUND THE RIM AND THE BODY IS LEAD IN THE FORM OF DRIPPING ICICLES," EXPLAINS KAZARIAN, "AND THE SPOUT IS IN THE FORM OF A SERPENT."

**RIGHT**  KAZARIAN'S RULE WHEN DECORATING HIS HOME IS "TO BREAK DOWN THE BOUNDARIES OF AGE OR PLACE OF ORIGIN," AS HE SAYS. "I COULDN'T TAKE MORE PLEASURE THAN IN PUTTING A FRENCH ART DECO PIECE NEXT TO AN EIGHTEENTH-CENTURY PIECE." A STARTLING FOCUS IN THIS IDIOSYNCRATIC ROOM IS THE GILDED WEATHERVANE IN THE SHAPE OF A COD THAT SITS IN FRONT OF THE WINDOW TO CATCH THE SUNSHINE. IN THE CENTER OF THE ROOM IS A STONE POND, WITH BRONZE FIGURES OF THE PAGAN GOD, PAN, ON EITHER SIDE, EACH TRYING TO LURE THE OTHER ACROSS THE WATER.

**RIGHT ABOVE** THIS BEAUTIFULLY MADE CABINET IS AN EXAMPLE OF THE "BANKS" OF DRAWERS OR FILING CABINETS THAT DUTCH MERCHANTS TOOK TO THE DOCKS IN THE NINETEENTH CENTURY WHEN SHIPS WERE EXPECTED; THE COMMERCIAL EQUIVALENT OF CAMPAIGN FURNITURE. THE TRUNK IS ANOTHER ANTIQUE, MADE IN NEW ENGLAND IN 1826.

**RIGHT BELOW** IN THIS BEDROOM, KAZARIAN HAS INDULGED HIS TASTE FOR PUTTING FURNITURE FROM DIFFERENT ERAS IN THE SAME SPACE, "BREAKING DOWN BOUNDARIES" AS HE PUTS IT. HERE A 1920s STEEL DESK COMPLEMENTS A NINETEENTH-CENTURY DUTCH BENCH. KAZARIAN LOVES THE BENCH BECAUSE "IT HAS THE QUALITIES WE ASSOCIATE WITH A PIECE OF SCULPTURE, MORE THAN THE QUALITIES WE ASSOCIATE WITH A PLACE TO SIT."

**OPPOSITE** A STUDY OF STRIPES: IN THE GUEST ROOM, A NINETEENTH-CENTURY FRENCH BRASS CAMPAIGN BED LOOKS COZY, AND FAR MORE COMFORTABLE THAN MANY MODERN BEDS DESIGNED TO LAST FOR LONGER THAN A SWIFT MILITARY CAMPAIGN. A SWATH OF ORANGE AND GRAY STRIPED FABRIC HANGS FROM THE TOP OF THE FOUR-POSTER BED AS A BACKDROP. THE EXCESSIVE NUMBER OF PILLOWS ADD TO THE GENERAL ATMOSPHERE OF COMFORT AND EASE. THE STRIPED MOTIF REPEATS ITSELF IN THE BLUE COMFORTER AND THE NINETEENTH-CENTURY VELLUM TRUNK. "IT'S ASTONISHING THAT PEOPLE WOULD GO TO BATTLEFIELDS WITH BRASS BEDS AND MAHOGANY CHESTS," KAZARIAN SAYS. "THERE MUST HAVE BEEN A HUGE SERVANT CLASS THERE TO SERVE RATHER THAN FIGHT."

**LEFT** THE OBJECTS IN THE NEWLY-
RENOVATED SECOND-FLOOR BATHROOM
HAVE BEEN ARRANGED AS IF
IN A GALLERY. THEY ARE PRECISE,
PROVOCATIVE, AND INVITE PROLONGED
STUDY. THE FADED PAINTED
WOOD MEDICINE CABINET HARMONIZES
WITH THE PAINTED WOOD BALUSTERS
BENEATH. ABOVE THE SINK,
KAZARIAN HAS JUXTAPOSED A 1950s
RUBBER MERMAID BOAT BUMPER
WITH A NINETEENTH- CENTURY ENGLISH
SHAVING MIRROR. BOTH THE
MERMAID AND THE MIRROR APPEAR TO
SIGNIFY VANITY. TOWELS ARE
ARRANGED JUST SO. ONE IS DRAPED OVER
A PIECE OF FURNITURE TO
THE RIGHT OF THE SINK.
EXTRAS ARE FOLDED AND STACKED
NEATLY TO THE RIGHT AT
THE BACK OF THE ROOM. A BLEACHED SKULL
HANGS ON THE
WALL ABOVE A FADED WHITE STRIP OF
WOOD, WHICH ALSO FUNCTIONS
AS A SHALLOW SHELF FOR
AN ARRAY OF SHAVING BRUSHES WHICH,
SIMPLY BY BEING ARRANGED
TOGETHER, SEEM TO MERIT MORE THAN
AN ORDINARY GLANCE. AS AN ANTIQUES
DEALER, KAZARIAN KNOWS THE GRAPHIC
STRENGTH OF GROUPING LIKE WITH LIKE.

**RIGHT** IN AN UNUSED CORNER
OF THE BATHROOM, KAZARIAN HAS
CREATED A TABLEAU OF
NINETEENTH - AND TWENTIETH-CENTURY
OBJECTS, UNITED BY THEIR
WORN, MOTTLED SURFACES AND STRONG,
ANGULAR SHAPES. EACH
OBJECT HAS ITS OWN HUMBLE PATINA.

"I like big and bold," says Francine Gardner, who, with Laurent Kriegel, owns Interieurs, a Manhattan home furnishings store. "I like mountains. I like expanses of land." Francine shares a 6,500 square-foot 1920s former stable house with her husband, Luke Gardner, a lawyer, and their young children in Stamford, Connecticut. The U-shaped house, with an interior courtyard, is set in two acres of land. When they bought the house in 1990, she opened up the house, tore down all the non-supporting walls and re-configured the rooms, filling them with air and light. As a finishing touch she stripped off all the paint and ripped up the shag carpeting.

Everything she has designed, or bought for the house (and her store) is big, bold, and clean-lined. There is both a heightened sense of form (tall, squared-off armoires, big, chunky chests and tables) and sybaritic comfort

# FAMILY ECHOES

**OPPOSITE** GARDNER PAINTED HER HOME WHITE, A NEUTRAL BACKDROP FOR BOLDLY SCALED OBJECTS. THE ONLY DOMINANT COLOR IS THE TERRA COTTA TILED FLOOR. UNDER THE STAIRCASE AN OVERSCALED WOODEN BOWL BY JEROME ABEL SEGUIN SITS ON THE EIGHTEENTH-CENTURY AMERICAN PINE BLANKET CHEST.

**RIGHT** THE HOUSE IS U-SHAPED, WITH STABLES, SERVANTS' QUARTERS AND A SHED SET AROUND A COURTYARD. ALTHOUGH IT IS IN CONNECTICUT, IT REMINDED GARDNER OF A U-SHAPED FARM IN THE GASCOGNE REGION IN FRANCE CALLED A BASTIDE. HERE, A BIRDHOUSE SITS ON A WHITE WICKER TABLE.

throughout the house. Each capacious chair invites you to sit down and wrap yourself up one of the cashmere, chenille or wool throws that always happen to be a fingertip away. "Wherever I am, I like a big space around me," says Gardner, "and I use textiles to make me feel warm and safe." The textiles transform every chair, chaise, or sofa into a potential cocoon.

She neither wears or designs with bright colors. "I wear brown, black, and gray," she says, "and I find neutral colors calming." Most of the walls are white, and much of the floor is laid with 10-inch square Mexican clay tiles, stained the same shade of terra cotta red as the floors in her home in Clermont Dessous, a twelfth-century town in the Gascogne region of France. She has transplanted colors, memories, and heirlooms from her French home town to Connecticut, where she has filled the house with echoes not only of her family, but also of her husband's. The bird sculpture that hangs near the stairs once belonged to his family.

At one end of the living room, Gardner knocked down the sheetrock wall to expose an area that had once been a trough in the manger. A scalloped eighteenth-century Spanish fruitwood bench sits there now, and on the wall hang African sculptures collected by the Gardner family, and a painting by Leberdene, a Vietnamese artist.

Outdoors, the same pristine white prevails. The house is white, and so is the wicker furniture. The color in the surrounding environment comes from antique sixteenth-century English roses, wisteria, and ivy, and, in the Fall, the trees that blaze vermilion, canary, and tangerine.

**LEFT** GARDNER SPENDS MOST OF HER
RARE FREE TIME ALONE — WHEN
HER CHILDREN ARE IN FRANCE FOR A FEW
WEEKS EVERY SUMMER VISITING
HER PARENTS — READING ON THIS CHINTZ-
COVERED CHAISE. THE BEIGE LINEN
CURTAINS IN THIS ROOM ARE CUT EXTRA-
LONG SO THAT THEY TRAIL ON
THE FLOOR, GIVING A SIMPLE WINDOW
TREATMENT A TOUCH OF LUXURY.

**LEFT BELOW** A ROSARY THAT
BELONGED TO GARDNER'S
GREAT-GRANDMOTHER HANGS FROM A
POST, ANOTHER MEMORY OF FRANCE,
AND ESPECIALLY OF FAMILY.

**RIGHT** THE LIVING ROOM
IS AN EXPANSIVE, SOOTHING SPACE,
WHERE THE COOL WHITE OF
THE WALLS AND THE WHITE LINEN-COVERED
FURNITURE CONTRASTS WITH
THE WARM TERRA COTTA TILED FLOOR.
THE VAST COFFEE TABLE IS AN
OLD WORK TABLE WITH ITS LEGS CUT DOWN
TO SIZE. THE SCALLOP-BACKED
BENCH MAKES A FEATURE OF A NICHE THAT
USED TO BE A TROUGH. THE PREVIOUS
OWNER HAD COVERED IT WITH
SHEET ROCK, AND ONE DAY, IN A FRENZY
OF ENTHUSIASM, GARDNER TORE
IT ALL DOWN. "THEN I CALLED
IN SOMEONE TO FIX IT," SHE SAYS.

When Dennis Kyte, an artist, and Seymour Surnow, a real estate broker, bought a 1960s house in Washington, Connecticut, they decided to furnish it with pieces only by artists that they fell in love with. Kyte is the author of *The Botanical Footwork*, a collection of drawings depicting fantastical shoes made of flowers, vines and plants. He and his partner, Surnow, are not only inveterate and impassioned collectors, but they are also archivists. They know the provenance of each and every table, chair, desk, and lamp in the house. Anonymous furniture, thrift shop finds and hand-me-downs are not part of their vocabulary. The only piece of furniture which has no pedigree is the dining table – a massive Dutch farm table, whose date of origin, wood, and designer is unknown. What sold them was function. "We were told the table was solid enough to dance on," Kyte says.

# MODERN LIVING

The two men are primarily fans of twentieth-century modernists, like Charles and Ray Eames, Isamu Noguchi, Florence Knoll, Le Corbusier, and Harry Bertoia. But they are also devotees of Gaetano Pesce, the Italian architect who makes furniture, vases, and bowls of resin. "Pesce says rubber and resin will be the Venini glass of the future," says Kyte.

The house has high ceilings, enormous rooms, and is painted white throughout so that the furniture stands out as if in an art gallery, but the pieces are grouped in a friendly, residential fashion. Where there are chairs, there are also reading lights and tables for books and cups of coffee.

The most visually provocative objects in the house are brilliantly colored sideshow posters by Snap Wyatt, who painted performers at Riverview Park, near Chicago, in the Fifties. One, Olga the Snake Lady, is in Kyte's studio, where it dominates a cluster of four of Le Corbusier's Le Grand Confort chairs. The chairs are arranged in a square, but it is the 10-foot high red and yellow poster that lures the eye.

Even the furniture in the bathroom has a provenance. The towels are stacked on Sori Yanagi's signed molded plywood butterfly chairs, designed in the Fifties. Big mercury glass balls from the Thirties are on one end of the tub. "They reflect the room," says Kyte, "and we're amused by things that are bright and shiny." Above the sink is a procession of objects: a fossilized stone snail, a Venini turquoise and white glass vase, and a clear sparkling square of a mysterious material. "It's deodorant," says Kyte. Even the most banal necessities are chosen for their beauty.

**LEFT ABOVE AND BELOW** THE PRECISION APPLIED BY KYTE AND SURNOW TO THEIR FURNITURE IS EXTENDED TO THE LANDSCAPING OF THEIR GARDEN — WHICH IS, AFTER ALL, IN CONNECTICUT, WHERE THE RURAL GENTRY MANICURE THEIR LAWNS AS WELL AS THEIR HANDS. ALL SHRUBS AND TREES IN THIS ELEGANT YARD ARE CAREFULLY PRUNED AND SHAPED, AND THE GRASS IS WEED-FREE. EVEN THE DOGS, VIZSLA HUNGARIAN POINTERS NAMED ROWBOAT (LEFT) AND RABBIT (RIGHT), DRAPE THEMSELVES LANGUIDLY OVER A STONE "SOFA" AND ADD TO THE GENERAL ATMOSPHERE OF WELL-BRED CHIC.

**RIGHT** THE DINING ROOM IS THE ONLY SPACE WITH ANY ANONYMOUS ANTIQUE PIECES, CHOSEN FOR THEIR FUNCTION AND EXAGGERATED SCALE. THE DUTCH FARM TABLE IS SO STURDY THAT KYTE WAS ASSURED THAT HE COULD DANCE ON IT. HE ADDED A SMALL MIRROR TO THE OVERSCALED FAN SO THAT LIGHT COULD REFLECT FROM ABOVE THE DOUBLE DOORS. BUT HIS FAVORITE PIECE IN THIS SPACE IS THE GILDED FIBERGLASS ALLIGATOR THAT DOMINATES THE TABLE. "I LIKE ALL JUNGIAN ARCHETYPES, AND I LOVE ANIMAL GODS," SAYS KYTE, WHO CHOSE THE CENTERPIECE.

**BELOW** HARRY BERTOIA'S WIRE CHAIRS SURROUND THE TABLE IN KYTE AND SURNOW'S KITCHEN. EVERYTHING IS CHOSEN FOR ITS ELEGANCE AND BEAUTY. EVEN THE KITCHEN LADDER IS NOT FOR CLAMBERING UP AND DOWN TO CHANGE THE LIGHT BULB — IT IS AN ART PIECE BY DANIEL MACK, AN AMERICAN DESIGNER WHO FIRST BECAME FAMOUS FOR HIS TWIG FURNITURE. THE PLASTER TABLE IS A PIECE BY JOHN DICKINSON, WHOSE COMPANY KYTE AND SURNOW USED TO OWN. DICKINSON WAS FAMOUS FOR DESIGNING TABLES AND CONSOLES WITH ANIMAL LEGS. "THEY'RE CLOSE TO AFRICAN STOOLS," SAYS KYTE.

**ABOVE** A FIREPLACE WARMS THE MASTER BEDROOM, WHICH, LIKE THE REST OF THE HOUSE, IS FURNISHED WITH TWENTIETH-CENTURY MODERNIST CLASSICS. IN THE 1970s, WHEN KYTE AND SURNOW LIVED IN SAN FRANCISCO, THEY COLLECTED THE ART OF THE INSANE. "IT WAS VISUALLY CHAOTIC," SAYS KYTE. AFTER THEY SOLD THE COLLECTION, THEY DECIDED TO CHOOSE ONLY ART AND FURNITURE THAT OFFERED THEM TRANQUILITY.

**ABOVE** WHEN THE COUPLE LIVED IN SAN FRANCISCO, THEY BOUGHT JOHN DICKINSON'S COMPANY, WHICH THEY EVENTUALLY SOLD. WHAT THEY RETAIN, HOWEVER, IS A COLLECTION OF THE DESIGNER'S FURNITURE, INCLUDING THE LACQUERED PLASTER TABLE WITH A ROPE WRAPPED AROUND IT. NEATLY ROLLED TOWELS REST ON SORI YANAGI'S 1950s WOOD BUTTERFLY STOOL, WHICH IS ALSO IN THE MUSEUM OF MODERN ART IN MANHATTAN.

**RIGHT** THIS ASTONISHING CIRCUS POSTER, "TURKEY BOY" BY SNAP WYATT, ACTS AS A HEADBOARD. WYATT WAS ONE OF AMERICA'S MOST FAMOUS SIDESHOW POSTER ARTISTS IN THE 1950s AND 1960s. THE BED COVERINGS ARE MORE SUBDUED — THE BEDSPREAD IS A WOVEN TAPESTRY BY ANICHINI, A MAKER OF BEAUTIFUL ITALIAN LINENS. THE WHITE SHEETS AND PYRAMID OF PILLOWS ACT AS A SOOTHING COUNTERPOINT TO THE POSTER.

Bunny Williams's Federal house originally belonged to Eban Brewster, who built it in 1840. Brewster was a prosperous farmer and his house was set on hundreds of acres of land of which Williams now owns 25. The house is on a country road, but set back 150 feet. She bought it in 1978 as an escape from hectic Manhattan. Williams loved the landscape, but she also discovered that the people of the town were social activists. Before she bought the house, she spent a weekend in a nearby inn. "In front of the inn was a line of people with banners campaigning for nuclear disarmament," she says. "They were there every weekend."

In 1990, Williams, a well-respected interior designer, and her partner John Rosselli, visited the Chelsea Flower Show in London. This inspired them to open a garden furniture shop called Treillage in Manhattan, where

# GARDEN COLOR

OPPOSITE EBAN BREWSTER,
THE ORIGINAL OWNER OF THIS 1840S
FEDERAL HOUSE, MARRIED
A WOMAN FROM NATCHEZ, MISSISSIPPI,
AND TO MAKE HER FEEL
AT HOME HE ADDED A DOUBLE
LATTICE PORCH THAT WRAPPED
AROUND TWO FLOORS.

RIGHT THE FORMER MANOR HOUSE IS
TYPICAL OF FEDERAL HOUSES IN THE AREA,
BUILT OF WOOD, WITH FANLIGHTS
ABOVE THE DOOR
AND PAINTED WHITE OUTSIDE. BREWSTER
BUILT THE HOUSE AS AN ADDITION
TO PROPERTY BUILT
IN THE EIGHTEENTH CENTURY.

they sell antiques and antique reproductions from England, France, and the United States. Landscape and gardens are very important to Williams and she designed her house to bring the outdoors in. Since she is not an architectural purist, she expanded the house, tearing down walls, re-configuring rooms, and installing large windows in the kitchen, and floor-to-ceiling arched windows in the barn. The huge windows blur the boundaries between inside and out. Although she has plants and flowers throughout the house, she has also created a winter garden, a conservatory, in the barn. "By building this big glass room to hold tender plants, we can have passion flowers and jasmine into the winter," she says. "And during the day, it's warm and toasty." The conservatory, she says, is not an old New England tradition. It developed in the nineteenth century when plate glass became available. Williams's design principles are guided by the fact that she does not furnish a room by period. Instead, she mixes eighteenth-and nineteenth-century antiques from Europe and America, juxtaposing cultures and periods, so that there is always something unique and intriguing to look at. But behind her design is a concern for comfort. As an interior designer, she is always careful to ensure that there is somewhere for people to put down their drink or book. She places a reading light by every easy chair. There is not a white room in the house and each room is painted a different color. The long New England winter extends from November into April and Williams finds the idea of white rooms in a white landscape bleak.

**LEFT** WILLIAMS AND ROSSELLI ALSO OWN
TREILLAGE, A MANHATTAN SHOP
SPECIALIZING IN GARDEN FURNITURE.
THEY TRY TO BRING THE OUTDOORS
INDOORS, AS IN THE CONSERVATORY,
WHERE THEY HAVE SURROUNDED THIS LACY
BIRDCAGE WITH FLOWERING PLANTS.

**RIGHT** THE BARN HAS BEEN
TRANSFORMED INTO A HOUSE, INCLUDING A
CONSERVATORY-DINING ROOM.
WHEN WILLIAMS FOUND THE THREE ARCHED
WINDOWS, WHICH ARE 32 FEET LONG,
SHE KNEW IMMEDIATELY WHERE TO PUT
THEM: ALONG THE 32-FOOT LONG WALL
OF THE BARN. THE PLANTS SOAR FROM
FLOOR TO CEILING, GIVING THE ROOM
THE AMBIENCE AND FRAGRANCE
OF A GREENHOUSE.

**OPPOSITE** A HIGH-BACKED CHAIR,
A TALL LAMP, AND PLANTS MAKE THIS
WRITING TABLE A SEDUCTIVE PLACE
TO COMPOSE A LETTER. WILLIAMS DESIGNED
THE POLISHED WAX CONCRETE FLOOR,
OF FOUR-FEET SQUARES SET IN THIN WOOD
FRAMES, FOR RADIANT HEATING,
SINCE THERE IS NO BASEMENT IN
WHICH TO PUT A FURNACE.

ABOVE THIS TINY ROOM OPENS OFF THE
CONSERVATORY-DINING ROOM IN THE BARN,
AND IS USED TO STORE GARDENING
ACCOUTREMENTS. WILLIAMS FINDS THE
ENORMOUS STONE SINK USEFUL IN THE
UPKEEP OF HER WINTER GARDEN.

**LEFT**  IN THE EIGHTEENTH CENTURY,
NEW ENGLAND HOMES HAD TINY MULLIONS
TO LET IN LIGHT BUT PREVENT HEAT
FROM LEAVING THE HOUSE.
WILLIAMS, HOWEVER, EXPANDED THE
KITCHEN BY SIX FEET AND
INSTALLED A LARGE WINDOW. THE LIGHT
NOW REACHES SO FAR INTO THE INTERIOR
THAT IT ILLUMINATES THE ITALIAN
CANE-BACKED DINING CHAIRS AND ENGLISH
TUDOR FRUITWOOD TABLE.
WILLIAMS KNOWS JUST HOW
TO CREATE AN INVITING, COMFORTABLY
VOLUPTUOUS ROOM SETTING.
NEXT TO HER NEW KITCHEN WINDOW,
SHE HAS PLACED A 1920S FRENCH LEATHER
SOFA, WITH SOFT PILLOWS TO
MAKE IT A COMFORTABLE PLACE FOR
READING UNDER THE CANOPY OF THE TREE.
THE VICTORIAN HIGH-BACKED CHAIR PLACED
NEARBY MAKES IT A PERFECT PLACE FOR
CONVERSATION AS WELL.

**RIGHT**  GARDNER'S SENSE OF COMFORT IS
OMNIPRESENT, WHETHER INDOORS OR
OUT, AND THIS BENCH IS PERFECT
FOR CHATTING IN THE GARDEN.

Gretchen Mann, an interior designer in Lyme, Connecticut, likes only big things. "Don't buy anything smaller than a cow," she says. Her husband, Mowry Mann, is a tall man – six foot, five inches to be exact – so all the furniture has to be in proportion to him to make him feel as comfortable as possible. And she applies this maxim to things both animate and inanimate – armoires, four-poster beds, chandeliers, even the finials. The focus of her furnishings is always upwards and she describes the cupboards, dovecote, and even topiaries as soaring towards the ceiling. She and Mowry Mann, a publisher of corporate histories, and their daughter, Molly, share an 1820s Federal house and nine acres of land in an old boat-building town in Connecticut with 83 animals, including eight dogs and 50 chickens (the only vertically-challenged objects allowed).

# BIG ON STYLE

Gretchen Mann discovered the answer to paw prints and dog hairs left all over her furnishings. "I covered all the chairs and sofas in vinyl or animal-print fabric," she says. Out went the white linen slipcovers, and in came vinyl, which can be scrubbed clean. Bed linens and coverings are cotton, floors are painted, and rugs are patterned. Background colors are creamy grays and beiges.

In summer, Mann doesn't have simple nosegays around the house. Instead, she uses topiaries, often of juniper. On the columned front porch she has topiaries in urns. "It's about presenting a pretty face," she says.

If topiaries are one of Mann's favorite decorating devices, so too are finials. She collects finials from the United States, England, and France. All are big, usually white, and they are grouped around the house, on the tops of mantels, bureaus, armoires, and cupboards. In the pale gray kitchen, with its granite counter, Mann has placed a zinc finial that in the late 1800s graced the roof of a barn in Vermont.

The dining room is a study of beige and white table and chairs accented with enormous objects. The pristine chandelier, with its sprays of tiny lamps with white shades, was once "disgustingly cheap, black Spanish wrought iron," Mann says. "I hung it from a tree and spray-painted it white, and wrapped fabric around the chain."

In the master bedroom, the walls are a pale gray and off-white, and the same muted color scheme shows up in the three zinc finials which perch on top of a Hudson River Valley cupboard, also pale gray.

**LEFT ABOVE**  THE DOGGY THEME
IS CONTINUED OUTSIDE, WHERE TWO DOG
STATUES AND TWO JUNIPER
STANDARDS GUARD A LITTLE-USED SIDE
DOOR ONTO THE LAWN.
"IT'S ABOUT PRESENTING A PRETTY
FACE," REMARKS MANN.

**LEFT BELOW**  THIS VIEW OF THE GARDEN
DEMONSTRATES MANN'S
PENCHANT FOR ALL THINGS LARGE.
THIS HUGE BIRD HOUSE, ON A
CORRESPONDINGLY TALL PEDESTAL,
ECHOES THE GENERAL SENSE OF SCALE
IN A GARDEN WHERE THE TOPIARY BY THE
HOUSE IS AS TALL AS THE WINDOWS
AND WHERE EVEN THE GRASS IS TALL.

**RIGHT**  THE FAMILY SPENDS MOST OF
THEIR TIME DURING THE SHORT
CONNECTICUT SUMMER HANGING OUT BY
THE POOL. WHEN THEY AND THEIR FRIENDS
AREN'T SWIMMING, THEY CAN EAT OR
READ AT THIS TABLE SHADED BY
A CANVAS UMBRELLA. THE ADIRONDACK
CHAIRS ARE A COMMON FEATURE IN
NEW ENGLAND HOMES. UNUSUALLY FOR
OUTSIDE FURNITURE, THEY ARE DEEP,
CAPACIOUS, AND FAIRLY COMFORTABLE.
THE MANNS ALWAYS MAKE SURE THAT
THERE IS A HANDY SPOT TO PUT A GLASS OF
WINE FOR THOSE SUMMER EVENINGS
WHEN THE SUN FALLS SOFTLY ACROSS THE
PAVED AREA, A PLACE FOR
CONTEMPLATION AND RELAXATION.

**LEFT ABOVE** SINCE THE MANNS LIVE WITH SO MANY ANIMALS, THEY HAVE ONLY A FEW RUGS AND NO WALL-TO-WALL CARPETS. INSTEAD, THEY HAVE PAINTED FLOORS SO THAT THE DOG AND CAT HAIRS ARE EASILY VACUUMED OR SWEPT UP. BUT TO GIVE THE FLOORS VISUAL INTEREST, GRETCHEN HAS PAINTED THEM A CHECKERBOARD PATTERN.

**LEFT BELOW** THERE IS SCARCELY A WINDOW IN THE HOUSE THAT DOESN'T HAVE A PLANT OR TOPIARY IN FRONT OF IT, OR A PIECE OF FURNITURE WITHOUT A FINIAL ON TOP. GRETCHEN COLLECTS LARGE FINIALS AND PLACES THEM ON TOP OF TABLES, MANTELPIECES, SHELVES, AND, AS SHOWN HERE, ON CUPBOARDS.

**RIGHT** THE MANNS KNOCKED DOWN SOME OF THE WALLS OF THE ORIGINAL HOUSE TO MAKE MORE SPACIOUS ROOMS AND BRING IN MORE LIGHT AND AIR, BUT THEY LEFT THE ORIGINAL FLOOR INTACT AND GAVE IT A JACKSON POLLOCK-LIKE DRIZZLE OF PAINT ( A TRADITION IN THE REGION). THE CASUALLY SPLATTERED FLOOR IS IN THE MUD ROOM.

**BELOW** MANN'S PASSION FOR FINIALS
AND GREENERY IS DEMONSTRATED
HERE IN THE MUD ROOM,
WHERE A SENSE OF BALANCE IS ACHIEVED
BY THE SYMMETRY OF THE
ARRANGEMENT. THE BOOTS COLLECTED
UNDER THE TABLE ARE
MOSTLY FOR TRAMPING THROUGH THE
FIELDS, BUT SOME ARE RIDING BOOTS.
THE MANNS HAVE FOUR HORSES
AND HAVE BOUGHT A PONY
FOR THEIR DAUGHTER MOLLY.
MANN, HOWEVER, DOES NOT RIDE
WESTERN OR ENGLISH.
"I RIDE BAREBACK," SHE EXPLAINS.

**ABOVE** THE KITCHEN IS LARGE ENOUGH TO INCLUDE A COZY SITTING AREA. THE FAN ABOVE THE WORKING FIREPLACE DATES FROM AN 1860S FEDERAL HOUSE, WHERE IT PROBABLY ADORNED THE FRONT DOOR. THE ENORMOUS ZINC FINIAL ON THE LOW TABLE DATES FROM THE NINETEENTH CENTURY AND IS FROM VERMONT, WHERE IT MAY HAVE TOPPED THE ROOF OF A BARN. THE FURNITURE IS COVERED IN PET-PROOF VINYL.

**ABOVE** MORE OF MANN'S EXTENSIVE COLLECTION OF FINIALS ADORNS THE LEDGE IN THE LIVING ROOM. FABRIC THROWS AND TEXTURED PILLOWS ADD A FEELING OF WARMTH AND COMFORT TO THE VINYL SOFA AND THE VIVID COLORS OF THE CASUALLY ARRANGED ROSES AND PEONIES SEEM TO ATTRACT THE SUN AND CONTRAST WITH THE COOL WHITE ORNAMENTS IN THE SHADOWS BEHIND.

**OPPOSITE** THE EIGHTEETH-CENTURY GILDED WOODEN ROOSTER ONCE GRACED A TAVERN IN NEW HAMPSHIRE, AND IN A CORNER SITS A MASSIVE TIN DOVECOTE. THE OBJECT THAT MANN IS MOST PROUD OF, HOWEVER, IS THE CHANDELIER. IT WAS ORIGINALLY BLACK, BUT MANN SPRAY PAINTED IT WHITE TO BLEND IN BETTER WITH THE NEUTRAL COLOR SCHEME OF THE ROOM. THE LAMPS TILT AT DIFFERENT ANGLES, GIVING IT A WHIMSICAL AIR.

by the
S E A

The Wyeth family is an American artistic dynasty spanning three generations. N. C. Wyeth was an artist and illustrator, perhaps most famous for his drawings for the children's classics, and of his five children Andrew, who painted *Christina's World*, is a household name. Jamie, Andrew's son, works in oils like his grandfather, and paints Presidents and pigs, birdhouses and lighthouses, gulls and goats. This family's art style is realism, a near anachronism in an era of conceptual art, installation art, and performance pieces.

In 1978, Betsy Wyeth, Andrew's wife, saw the lighthouse on Southern Island, bought and restored it. They sold it in 1990, to Jamie, who lives there most of the year and uses the adjacent house as his studio and workshop. Phyllis, Jamie Wyeth's wife, lives part of the time on Southern Island and partly in their house in Tenants Harbor. The closeness to nature

# THE LIGHTHOUSE

**OPPOSITE** IN THE LARGE HOUSE, WITH FLOOR-TO-CEILING WINDOWS OVERLOOKING THE WATER, THE WYETHS CAN GET A SHARPER VIEW OF SHIPS, GULLS, AND STORMS BREWING THROUGH JAMIE WYETH'S COLLECTION OF BINOCULARS. THE TALL BEIGE SET IS RUSSIAN AND THE OTHERS ARE GERMAN.

**RIGHT** A RAMP LEADS FROM THE BELLTOWER OF THE LIGHTHOUSE. THE LIGHTHOUSE WAS DESIGNED FOR A FAMILY, AND THE BEACON WAS ORIGINALLY FIRED WITH WHALE OIL.

on Southern Island inspires Jamie Wyeth, and being the sole owner of the island, he can work in near total isolation. He paints 90 percent of his work on Southern Island, and the rest in Chadds Ford, Pennsylvania, where the Wyeths also have a home.

The lighthouse, built in 1867 and used until 1933, stands at the mouth of Penobscot Bay, from which views of the sea and ships are uninterrupted. The staircase is steep and narrow, but worth the climb. From the old light room at the top, you can peer out of the window and gaze at the water, imagining tall-masted ships sailing towards the island, watching for the guiding beacon. The sea is a constant presence in the Wyeths' lives. Not only does it surround them, but it is reflected in the decor of both houses, where it is captured in motifs on walls and materials. Both houses are furnished entirely with antiques, bought from various shops in Maine, Pennsylvania and Massachusetts. The furnishings are soft and gently worn with age – the Wyeths have deliberately chosen period decoration. They have a collection of hooked rugs, all depicting nautical themes – fish, sailors and boats, all perfect examples of American folk art – untutored, vivacious, and charming.

Throughout the interiors are casual still-lives, which are graphic, historic, and unaffected. At the desk in the watch room is a small telescope resting on an 1882 book called *Lights & Tides of the World,* which mentions the Southern Island lighthouse. A brass plaque in the house itself lists all the lighthouse keepers here from 1867 to 1933.

**LEFT** A COZY CORNER FOR PEOPLE TO WARM THEMSELVES BY THE BLAZING FIRE, READ A NEWSPAPER AND BE THANKFULFOR THE STURDY WALLS THAT SHUT OUT THE RAGING STORMS AND THE COLD.

**LEFT BELOW** THE WORN CHAIR IS A DELIBERATE ATTEMPT TO BE TRUE TO THE TRADITIONAL FEEL OF THE BUILDING, THE BOOK AN EXAMPLE OF JAMIE WYETH'S LOVE OF NATURE AND ARTISTIC STYLE.

**RIGHT** FROM 1867 TO 1933, WHEN THE LIGHTHOUSE WAS ACTIVE, THE LIVING ROOM WAS WHERE THE FAMILY GATHERED. THE TWO LEATHER SOFAS, WHICH WERE ISSUED BY THE UNITED STATES GOVERNMENT, OPEN UP INTO DOUBLE BEDS. THE CHAIRS ARE COVERED WITH SUMMER SLIPCOVERS, WHICH ARE BOTH COOL AND LIGHT. ALL THE FURNITURE IS WORN, WITH SOFT, MUTED COLORS. WYETH LIKES THE LOOK OF OLD PAINT, AND WILL OFTEN SCRAPE OFF THE TOP LAYER OF PAINT TO EXPOSE THE ORIGINAL COLOR. OLD HOOKED RUGS, MOSTLY WITH NAUTICAL THEMES, ARE SCATTERED ON THE FLOOR THROUGHOUT THE HOUSE.

OPPOSITE  THE DINING TABLE
IN THE LIGHTHOUSE AFFORDS A VIEW
OF THE WATER OF PENOBSCOT BAY.
THE TALL SLENDER LAMPS ON THE TABLE
ARE MADE FROM LIGHTNING RODS,
AND THE CLOCK IS FROM THE UNITED STATES
LIGHTHOUSE ESTABLISHMENT.

ABOVE RIGHT  AMERICA'S BEST-KNOWN
FAMILY OF PAINTERS ARE AS PROUD
OF THEIR COUNTRY AS THEIR COUNTRY IS
PROUD OF THEM, AND THIS
HAND-KNITTED STARS AND STRIPES
CUSHION DISPLAYS THEIR PATRIOTISM.
HANDWRITTEN LETTERS SCATTERED
AROUND ADD TO THE SENSE OF GRACEFUL
AGELESSNESS OF THE HOUSE.

RIGHT  IN THE WATCH ROOM
NINETEENTH-CENTURY ARTIFACTS ARE
DISPLAYED TO THEIR BEST ADVANTAGE ON
A PLAIN WHITE DESK AND CHAIR.
THE BOOK IS CALLED
LIGHTS & TIDES OF THE WORLD
AND FEATURES THE WYETHS' LIGHTHOUSE.

ABOVE  COLLECTIONS OF OBJECTS
AS DIVERSE AS TRADITIONAL
SCHOOL HATS AND NAVAL
PARAPHERNALIA HAVE BEEN HUNG
TOGETHER TO CREATE A CASUAL
YET ARTISTIC DISPLAY.

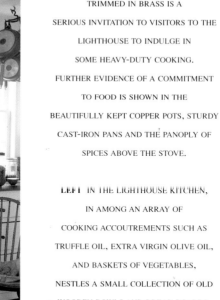

**ABOVE LEFT** A LA CORNUE STOVE
TRIMMED IN BRASS IS A
SERIOUS INVITATION TO VISITORS TO THE
LIGHTHOUSE TO INDULGE IN
SOME HEAVY-DUTY COOKING.
FURTHER EVIDENCE OF A COMMITMENT
TO FOOD IS SHOWN IN THE
BEAUTIFULLY KEPT COPPER POTS, STURDY
CAST-IRON PANS AND THE PANOPLY OF
SPICES ABOVE THE STOVE.

**LEFT** IN THE LIGHTHOUSE KITCHEN,
IN AMONG AN ARRAY OF
COOKING ACCOUTREMENTS SUCH AS
TRUFFLE OIL, EXTRA VIRGIN OLIVE OIL,
AND BASKETS OF VEGETABLES,
NESTLES A SMALL COLLECTION OF OLD
WOODEN BOWLS AND BREAD BOARDS,
BLEACHED FROM LONG USE.
TO THE RIGHT OF THE BOWLS IS A
CONTAINER FOR A COMPASS.

**RIGHT** IN THE BIG HOUSE,
THIS LONG, LOW SET OF WIDE DRAWERS
RUNS ALONG THE LENGTH OF
THE WALL, A CAPACIOUS PLACE FOR
STORAGE AS WELL AS FOR DISPLAY.
TINY BUCKETS IN DIFFERENT FADED COLORS
PROVIDE AN UNUSUAL FOCUS, AND
A SELECTION OF ART BOOKS
ARE CONVENIENTLY STORED
BENEATH THE DRAWERS.

Ainslie Gardner moved into her 10-bedroom, nineteenth-century property in 1985. This is her third family home in Newport, Rhode Island; her choice of house has always been based on the size of her family. Originally a farmhouse, it was partly renovated in the early nineteenth century by George Champlin Mason, a former reporter for the *Newport Mercury* turned architect. Between 1850 and 1950, the house was altered around 18 times, transforming slowly into an elegant summer house. A porch designed by Mason was added in around 1860, a High Victorian-style library around 1870, and a Federal Revival dining room just before 1900. These "exuberant additions" to the house were what caught Gardner's eye and she quickly added her own – she renovated it as soon as she bought it, ripping out all the plumbing, and moving every bathroom to different locations as well as installing new ones.

# A FAMILY AFFAIR

The key focus of the renovation was her family's needs. Her eldest grandchild has asthma, so she left the wood floors bare and now the children scamper freely from the house to the lawn and back again. There is a kitchen on the third floor, so that food for the babies can be prepared without disturbing the preparation of the grown-up meals. A large summer dining room can seat the entire family, and a smaller winter dining room also doubles as a sitting room. All the fireplaces in the house are fully functional as well as highly decorative. The house combines family comfort with the amenities of a very gracious style of living.

A mix of eighteenth-, nineteenth-, and early twentieth-century antiques from America, Italy, and England are tastefully arranged, but the absence of rugs makes the home and the furnishings appear less formal. In her master bedroom, a pair of Louis Seize-style chairs flank a round table, but rather than seeming ostentatious, they simply look low-slung and comfortable. Gardner also designed each room, deftly using color to create a special ambience in each one. The winter dining room is full of warm colors: the walls are painted terra cotta, while the fireplace has a wood mantel and a Delft blue surround. The library walls are a rich green, and Gardner has grouped a mix of nineteenth-century American wing chairs and a nineteenth-century English ladderback chair around the fireplace. None of these styles match, but this was a deliberate decision by Gardner to create a less formal look. Instead she has co-ordinated and united the eclectic collection of chairs by upholstering them all in the same fabric.

**LEFT** GARDNER BELIEVES
THAT WHERE THERE ARE CHILDREN, THERE
SHOULD BE THINGS TO PROVOKE
THEIR CURIOSITY. SHE PUT A
NINETEENTH-CENTURY MEDICAL SCALE ON
THE SECOND-FLOOR LANDING.
"IT'S THERE SO THE CHILDREN CAN ALL
WEIGH THEMSELVES AND FIND
OUT HOW TALL THEY ARE," SHE SAYS. COLOR
LITHOGRAPHS OF
AMERICAN INDIANS ARE ON THE WALL.
THEY ARE AS OLD AS THE HOUSE AND WERE
MADE BY EUROPEAN ARTISTS FOR
PUBLICATION IN A BOOK.

**LEFT BELOW** WHEN GARDNER DESIGNED
THE NEW BATHROOMS, SHE INSTALLED OLD
FIXTURES LIKE THESE IN A GUEST
BATHROOM OFF THE FIRST FLOOR. THE
PEDESTAL BASIN ADDS A TOUCH
OF ELEGANCE TO THIS MUTED AREA.

**OPPOSITE** THE HOUSE HAS TWO DINING
ROOMS. THE SUMMER DINING ROOM
IS VERY LARGE, AND CAN
ACCOMMODATE LARGE PARTIES.
THIS MUCH SMALLER ROOM, WITH THE
BLUE FIREPLACE, IS THE MORE
INTIMATE WINTER DINING ROOM AND
DOUBLES AS A SITTING ROOM.
THE HARDWOOD FLOORS ARE LEFT
BARE TO KEEP THE HOUSE AS
DUSTFREE AS POSSIBLE, ESPECIALLY FOR
GARDNER'S GRANDCHILD WHO
HAS ASTHMA. BUT THE BARE FLOORS
ALSO MAKE IT EASIER
FOR PEOPLE TO RUN ABOUT BAREFOOT
IN THE SUMMER, AND ADD
A SENSE OF EASE AND CASUALNESS TO
THIS ELEGANT HOME.

Ronald Lee Fleming, an architect in Cambridge, Massachusetts, owns a 1910 Federal Revival house on Bellevue Avenue in Newport, Rhode Island, designed by Ogden Codman Jr., the co-author with Edith Wharton of *The Decoration of Houses* (1897).

He is the third owner of this grand house, with its rotunda, spectacular circular staircase and 10 bedrooms. However, though large, the house is still on a residential scale, "Codman was a master of taking proportions he'd measured in France, England, and America and composing the pieces to a particular, very domestic scale," says Fleming, who has been a trustee of the Society for the Preservation of New England Antiquities.

The three-story wooden house is formal yet airy, suffused with light and breeze. On entering through a columned door, the drama of the house is instant. You cross the threshold into the circular lobby, step onto the

# A GRAND SCALE

intricately laid marble floor, and look up towards the rotunda, where the lacy staircase delineates the space. Light streams through the skylit rotunda and casts shadows across the marble floor. The decorative plaster design on the walls is echoed in the carved wood of the chairs that flank the doors.

An arched, wood-paneled door leads into the drawing room, whose bay windows face the south, with a view of a fountain across a lawn. Two glass conservatories, or what Ronald Fleming likes to call "light boxes," flank the drawing room so that light cuts through the house.

Since the summers are humid, Codman designed the house so that breezes would filter through. Above the entrance is a fanlight, which swings open (if someone clambers up a ladder). A second door that opens onto the foyer has a glass top decorated in metal scrollwork, which swings open, like a Dutch door, so fresh air blows in. Codman was a pragmatic architect; "He understood the weather," Fleming says, "and he was very sensitive to practical engineering details. All the pipes and electrical wiring are in larger pipes in the basement, so you don't have to break into a wall. It's all forced air heating, and it was state of the art, at the time."

For privacy's sake, the bedrooms have curtains at the floor-to-ceiling windows, fireplaces for coziness, chaises for curling up and reading. In one of the main bedrooms, an eighteenth-century painting is set in a dramatic frame, designed like a broken pediment above the fireplace. In a second bedroom, an oval mirror, set horizontally, sits above the fireplace. As in the rest of the house, these dramatic focal points appear effortless.

**LEFT** EVERY ROOM IN THE HOUSE REFLECTS CODMAN'S STYLE OF DESIGN. HE HAD STRICT VIEWS AS TO "APPROPRIATENESS," AND WOULD NEVER HANG A LARGE PAINTING LIKE THIS EIGHTEENTH-CENTURY ONE IN ITS BROKEN PEDIMENT FRAME AGAINST A BACKGROUND OF PATTERN. "THE OVERLAYING OF PATTERN IS ALWAYS A MISTAKE," HE SAID.

**RIGHT** CODMAN BELIEVED IN SYMMETRY, AND IN THIS HIGHLY CIVILIZED BEDROOM THERE IS A GREAT SENSE OF BALANCE. CODMAN SAID THAT THE FIREPLACE WAS THE HEARTH, AND LOGICALLY THE PLACE WHERE PEOPLE WOULD WANT TO GATHER. THE CHAISE AND THE READING LIGHT ARE IN THE MOST OBVIOUS, INVITING PLACE: IN THE CORNER, SURROUNDED BY NATURAL LIGHT. WHEN HE DESIGNED A ROOM, LIKE THIS ONE, WITH A DADO, CORNICE, AND OVER-MANTEL, HE SUGGESTED THAT THE REST OF THE WALL BE PAINTED ONE COLOR AND LEFT UNORNAMENTED. CODMAN PRACTICED WHAT HE AND EDITH WHARTON PREACHED IN THEIR 1897 BOOK *THE DECORATION OF HOUSES*.

Cam and Gardiner Dutton are Nantucket people. Gardiner Dutton was once the CEO of two companies in Phoenix, Arizona, while his wife, Cam, was a clinical psychologist. Now they sell antiques, mostly eighteenth- and nineteenth-century American quilts, furniture, and decorative objects, in their store, Nantucket Country. They used to spend summers in Nantucket, fleeing the 115°F heat of an Arizona summer. Then they moved to Nantucket full-time, and in 1982 bought a nineteenth-century house, formerly belonging to a Quaker.

Gardiner has always collected art and Cam has always collected antiques. Together, they have blended their passions in their home and the shop. The focus of their collections (and home) is Americana, sometimes narrowed down to Nantucket. The scale of the furniture and objects complement the small windows and small rooms of their house. Quakers

# LIVING HISTORY

OPPOSITE IN THE LIBRARY, WHICH HAS THE ORIGINAL FIREPLACE, THE WINDOWS OVER THE DOOR ARE VISIBLE. QUAKERS BELIEVED THAT THERE OUGHT TO BE A WINDOW FOR GOD TO PEER IN WHENEVER HE WANTED. AN AMERICAN IMPRESSIONIST PAINTING OF A DORY, PROBABLY DATING FROM THE LATE NINETEENTH CENTURY, HANGS ON THE WALL.

RIGHT A COLLECTION OF CANES, MANY OF WHICH HAVE WHALEBONE HEADS, DATING FROM THE EIGHTEENTH AND NINETEENTH CENTURY, REST IN AN ANTIQUE CHINESE PORCELAIN UMBRELLA STAND, A SOUVENIR OF THE CHINA TRADE.

were the predominant religious group from the early eighteenth century, and the Duttons have furnished the house not unlike the way it might have been in the 1850s. Most of the floors are natural wood, but the living room floor is blue-gray spattered paint, a common Nantucket finish since the late 1800s when the whaling industry died. People painted the floor with deck paint and then sealed it. "It was a poor man's rug," says Cam.

Throughout the house, Cam Dutton has scattered pieces from her extensive quilt collection. Over the railing on the second-floor stair landing is a cobalt blue and white quilt called Delectable Mountains. On an American Victorian white iron bed is a Wandering Foot, while across the end of the same bed is a Double Wedding Variation, another cobalt blue and white quilt. The quilts do double duty: they are functional folk art.

Like many New Englanders, Cam Dutton is enamored of old painted furniture, and acquires pieces just because she likes the patina. In the living room she has an old 1840s farm bench that doubles as a coffee table, which she bought because of the paint: "almost a deep robin's-egg blue," she says. The Duttons have created a country ambience, a mix of family furniture, antiques, and new chairs and sofas upholstered in richly colored fabrics, such as a red and white plaid. For a mural by the staircase, they commissioned Kolene Spicher, a folk artist in Pennsylvania, to paint a scene of a junk in the port of Canton. But though the Duttons' house reflects the exoticism of American expeditions, it is quintessentially an American country house: at the front door, they fly an American flag.

**RIGHT TOP** "I NEVER SET OUT TO BE A DECORATOR," SAYS CAM DUTTON. "I DON'T WANT A STILTED LOOK. I HAVE FAMILY FURNITURE AND WE'LL KIND OF MIX THEM." THIS GROUPING OF SLIGHTLY DISPARATE OBJECTS PROVES HER POINT: A BASKET AND GLASSES HANG CASUALLY ABOVE A SPINDLY LEGGED PIG AND NEXT TO A FAT WHITE CHICKEN.

**RIGHT BOTTOM** ONE OF CAM DUTTON'S MANY COLLECTIONS: ROLLING PINS FROM ENGLAND AND THE UNITED STATES, WHICH SHE HAS ARRANGED CASUALLY USING GARDEN TWINE. THE WHOLE DUTTON FAMILY LOVES TO COOK; THE DUTTONS' SON JEFFREY AND HIS WIFE, SHARI, ARE BOTH CHEFS AND OWNERS OF "THE DAILY BREADS" IN NANTUCKET, AND CAM HERSELF LOVES TO COLLECT THE ACCOUTREMENTS OF HER PASSION.

**OPPOSITE** THE SIGN THAT SAYS "BELOVED" HAS AN INTERESTING HISTORY. "IT'S AN ANTIQUE QUARTERBOARD, WHICH CAME FROM SHIPS, AND WHICH PEOPLE USED TO NAME THEIR HOUSES," CAM DUTTON SAYS. HER HUSBAND GAVE HER THE QUARTERBOARD, SHE SAYS, "BECAUSE HE KNEW I LOVED THE ISLAND SO MUCH." ROLLING PINS ARE DISPLAYED HORIZONTALLY ON THE WALL ABOVE THE GROUP HANGING ON ROPE. ALTHOUGH THE ROUND PINE DATES FROM THE NINETEENTH CENTURY, THE TWO CHAIRS ARE NEW. "THEY'RE CONTEMPORARY COPIES OF OLD SHAKER CHAIRS," SAYS CAM DUTTON, WHOSE PASSION FOR ANTIQUES FADES AWAY WHEN IT COMES TO CHAIRS. "I PREFER NEW CHAIRS BECAUSE THEY HOLD UP BETTER FOR EVERYDAY USE," SHE SAYS. "OLD CHAIRS ARE RICKETY — I HAD A GUEST WHO CRUSHED AN ANTIQUE CHAIR." THE RARE ANTIQUE CHAIR THAT MAKES IT TO THEIR HOME IS USED SOLELY AS AN ACCENT PIECE.

When Jeffrey Naftulin, a lawyer, and his wife, Judy, an antiques dealer and interior designer, bought a lot in Chappaquiddick, Massachusetts, they wanted to combine the old with the new. To achieve this, they installed items from the eighteenth to the early twentieth centuries in a modern, understated summer house that overlooks Nantucket Sound. They asked Mark Hutker, an architect in nearby Vineyard Haven, to use one of the most common vernacular styles in New England and design a cedar shingle house with two separate wings connected by a breezeway. "We wanted it to be part of the landscape, to keep it low to the land," says Judy Naftulin. To bring the outside inside, she asked the architect to design floor-to-ceiling windows in some of the rooms. And to entice you outside, there is an enormous porch. The family sails, swims, scallops, and windsurfs in front of their home.

# MODERN CLASSIC

Judy Naftulin's interior design involved having as little color as possible. "I wanted a very neutral, soothing, cool environment," she said. Against the white walls, she has arranged her collections, which are not chosen for their age, nor for their provenance, but for their form, texture, and color. In a sun-filled hallway lined with windows, Naftulin created a tableau of two 1930s French, brown leather club chairs, near an 1910 painting by an artist from the Woodstock, New York school. A 100-year-old terra cotta oil pot, white with age, is perched on a stand. The dining area, surrounded by glass windows, faces the Nantucket Sound. The round table is a nineteenth-century oak clawfoot painted white. Naftulin tends to treat antiques in a slightly unusual way, improvising to make them just a little more practical and a bit more modern. In the kitchen, she added industrial casters to a French baker's table to create a work table of the right height. She wanted to use a nineteenth-century English campaign table for a writing desk, and added a drawer for usefulness. A collection of fish baskets hang on the wall above the desk. "They're from Morecambe, a coastal town in England," she says. "It was a promotional thing. They would wrap fish in newspapers, and put them in straw baskets." Mail, not fish, now goes into the baskets.

In the living room, however, with its soaring 18-foot-high ceiling, the Naftulins used enormous objects to punctuate the space. An oversized sofa covered in white denim faces the working fireplace, which is flanked by fluted nineteenth-century wood pilasters from a Southern mansion.

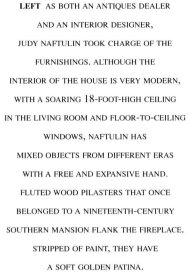

**LEFT** AS BOTH AN ANTIQUES DEALER AND AN INTERIOR DESIGNER, JUDY NAFTULIN TOOK CHARGE OF THE FURNISHINGS. ALTHOUGH THE INTERIOR OF THE HOUSE IS VERY MODERN, WITH A SOARING 18-FOOT-HIGH CEILING IN THE LIVING ROOM AND FLOOR-TO-CEILING WINDOWS, NAFTULIN HAS MIXED OBJECTS FROM DIFFERENT ERAS WITH A FREE AND EXPANSIVE HAND. FLUTED WOOD PILASTERS THAT ONCE BELONGED TO A NINETEENTH-CENTURY SOUTHERN MANSION FLANK THE FIREPLACE. STRIPPED OF PAINT, THEY HAVE A SOFT GOLDEN PATINA.

**LEFT** JUDY NAFTULIN LIKES TO PLAY WITH ANTIQUES AND MAKE THEM JUST SLIGHTLY DIFFERENT FROM THEIR ORIGINAL INTENT. SHE FOUND A NINETEENTH-CENTURY CLAWFOOT OAK TABLE AND PAINTED IT WHITE SO THAT THE CORNER DINING AREA WOULD GLOW FROM THE SUNLIGHT. THE TABLE HAS LEAVES, ALSO PAINTED WHITE, THAT MAKE IT ADJUSTABLE.

**OPPOSITE** MOST PEOPLE DRYDOCK THEIR BOATS IN WINTER. THE NAFTULINS TURNED THEIRS — A 1970s COPY OF A MAINE ISLAND GUIDE CANOE — UPSIDE DOWN, AND SUSPENDED IT ON STEEL RODS FROM THE CEILING. "IT ANCHORS THE CEILING TO THE FLOOR," JUDY NAFTULIN EXPLAINS. ALTHOUGH THE NAFTULINS SAIL, THEY NEVER USE THIS CANOE — IT IS SOLELY A DECORATIVE OBJECT. THE PIANO, HOWEVER, DOES HAVE ITS USES AND BOTH JUDY AND HER YOUNGER DAUGHTER PLAY.

**LEFT AND RIGHT** THE NAFTULINS'
ALL-WHITE HOME IS RICH WITH NATURAL
TEXTURES. THE CARELESSLY ARRANGED
BAMBOO BLINDS ALLOW UNEVEN
SHAFTS OF SUNLIGHT TO LIGHT UP THE
AREA WHERE FOOD PREPARATION
TAKES PLACE. THE VIEW FROM THE KITCHEN
WINDOW IS OF THE HERB
AND CUTTING GARDEN, PLANTED WITH
OREGANO AND THYME, ROSE HIPS
AND COSMOS, SUNFLOWERS, AND QUEEN
ANNE'S LACE. THE STURDY SQUARE
WORK TABLE IS A FRENCH BAKER'S TABLE.
WITH HER USUAL DISREGARD FOR
THE VENERATION WITH WHICH ANTIQUES
ARE GENERALLY HELD, NAFTULIN ADDED
INDUSTRIAL CASTERS TO THE LEGS OF THE
TABLE TO GIVE IT EXTRA HEIGHT, MAKING IT
EASIER TO WORK ON. SHE ALSO ADDED
A DRAWER TO THE NINETEENTH-CENTURY
ENGLISH CAMPAIGN TABLE.

**OPPOSITE** IN THE GUEST ROOM, AN ANONYMOUS EIGHTEENTH-CENTURY DUTCH PAINTING OF A GENTLEMAN LOOMS BY THE SIDE OF THE BED. JUDY NAFTULIN DELIGHTS IN ITS UNKNOWN PROVENANCE, AS IT NUDGES HER TO WONDER AND IMAGINE WHO AND WHAT THE SUBJECT WAS, AND WHAT KIND OF LIFE HE LIVED. "I LOVE DARK, BROODING PORTRAITS," SHE SAYS, "AND I PLAY THAT AGAINST THE MODERN BACKDROP. I LIKE THE OLD AND THE NEW."

**ABOVE RIGHT** JUDY NAFTULIN COULDN'T FIND A PAINTING TO FILL THE BARE EXPANSE OF WALL IN THE GUEST BATHROOM. SO SHE IMPROVISED AND HUNG FRENCH PLATES THAT WERE UNITED BY THEIR COLORS, RANGING FROM PALE CREAM TO BROWN AND WHITE.

**BELOW RIGHT** A MUTED. SOOTHING PALETTE OF TURQUOISE, BEIGE AND WHITE WAS CHOSEN FOR THE GUEST BEDROOM. THE PILLOWS ARE COVERED IN STURDY COTTON TICKING AND THE QUILT THROWN OVER THE BED IS ANTIQUE. SYMMETRY PREVAILS IN THIS ROOM. THERE ARE TWO ADJUSTABLE READING LAMPS WIRED INTO THE WALLS, AND NIGHT TABLES PLACED FOR CONVENIENCE ON EITHER SIDE OF THE BED.

**LEFT** THE BATHROOM AREA ADJOINING
THE MASTER BEDROOM
ALLOWS FOR SIDE-BY-SIDE ABLUTIONS:
DOUBLE SINKS, DOUBLE MIRRORS,
DOUBLE STORAGE. SINCE THE
FLOOR IS OF WOOD RATHER THAN
CONVENTIONALLY TILED,
"YOU CAN RUN AROUND BARE FOOT,"
WITHOUT BEING AFRAID OF SLIPPING
OVER AND BREAKING YOUR
NECK, AS JUDY NAFTULIN EXPLAINS.
AN ENGLISH STEEPING TUB
HAS BEEN PLACED IN FRONT OF A
WINDOW SO THAT WHOEVER IS
TAKING A BATH CAN GAZE OUT
ONTO THE WATER OUTSIDE.

**RIGHT** IN THE MASTER BEDROOM, THE BED
HAS BEEN CREATED AS A
SELF-CONTAINED ISLAND OF FURNITURE
DESIGNED FOR SLEEPING, READING, AND
STORAGE. WHAT APPEARS TO BE THE
HEADBOARD IS IN FACT A HANDY CABINET
OF BUILT-IN CLOTHES DRAWERS. ON TOP
OF THE CABINET IS A CARVED WOODEN
SWAN DECOY SURROUNDED BY AN
IDIOSYNCRATIC COLLECTION OF MORTARS
AND PESTLES. A FORTUNY LAMP,
DESIGNED LIKE A PHOTOGRAPHIC UMBRELLA
LAMP, IS IN THE CORNER OF THE
ROOM, A LARGE BLACK POLKA DOT
AGAINST THE WHITE WALLS. THE BAMBOO
BLINDS ENSURE THAT THIS IS ALWAYS
A LIGHT AND AIRY PLACE TO BE.

Constanze von Unruh, a German interior designer who lives in Nantucket in the summer, has a distinctive personal style. Whether working with an antique, a new fabric, or a contemporary chair, von Unruh treats everything with a modernist's hand. The scale is big. Lines are clean. Function is self-evident, and light and air proliferate. "I like big, clean statements," she says, "and a few whimsical silly things, or it gets overpowering." Her 1980s house in Nantucket is an airy 3,000-square-foot building filled with generous statements, combined with a touch of Shaker simplicity.

"The house is about gaining privacy within a Nantucket scheme," she says. The building codes there are strict, and homeowners cannot add on square footage willy-nilly. So von Unruh divided the house into communal areas – living room, kitchen, porch, and back yard – and private ones,

# COOL COUNTRY

**OPPOSITE** THE KITCHEN IS WHERE THE FAMILY GATHERS AND WHERE VON UNRUH, HER HUSBAND AND HER CHILDREN COOK. THE CEILING IS 16 FEET AT ITS HIGHEST POINT, SO THE 8-FOOT HIGH FRENCH PINE CUPBOARD FITS COMFORTABLY IN THE ROOM. THE DINING TABLE IS ALSO PINE AND IS SURROUNDED BY LLOYD LOOMS CHAIRS.

**RIGHT** VON UNRUH LIKES TO SURROUND HERSELF WITH SENSUOUS TEXTURES, FROM RAFFIA TO HORN TO RUSH. SHE ALSO LIKES MOMENTS OF SILLINESS. ON A STAIR LANDING, SHE HAS PLACED SOME MICKEY MOUSE BOWLING PINS TO LOOK AS IF THEY ARE CHATTING.

namely the upstairs bedrooms. Although the entire interior of the house is painted white, the range of surfaces she has used include sheetrock walls, wainscoting, and structural timbers to provide texture, shadows, and depth. The bleached floors enhance the whiteness of the house, while also suggesting the beach.

Texture is another von Unruh signature. She designed a raffia cloth, and draped it over a plain wood table, which is behind a sofa. By the windows facing the front porch, she put an old, anonymous French wood table and a sculptural, curvy cantilevered chair made of rush, and designed by Tom Dixon, the English furniture designer.

In the living room a sofa and an armchair are covered in a red and white Ralph Lauren striped fabric. Tossed over one of the sofas is a beautiful early twentieth-century French quilt, also red and white. The red, a shot of color in what is an all-white interior, is fresh and appealing. A cool north light floods in through the rear windows; the red, she says, "creates a bit of fire." To maximize the north light von Unruh has hung sheer organdie curtains, which flutter crisply in front of the windows. The frivolous elements in this room are three purely decorative raffia tassels, which dangle from the curtain rail.

The kitchen is the center of family life and everything in it is big. Once a garage, the room has a 16-feet high ceiling, which just happens to be the right height for the French cupboard. The cupboard may have been from a boarding school, but now it holds all the china, linens, and silverware.

**LEFT ABOVE** VON UNRUH IS FEARLESS ABOUT COLOR. IN THE COOL WHITE OF THIS EXPANSIVE LIVING ROOM, SHE HAS INSERTED A BRILLIANT SHOT OF RED. SHE HAS UPHOLSTERED THE SOFA AND ONE CHAIR IN A RALPH LAUREN RED AND WHITE STRIPED COTTON CANVAS, AND THEN TOSSED AN EARLY TWENTIETH-CENTURY RED AND WHITE FRENCH QUILT COVER OVER THE BACK OF THE SOFA. "THE RED GIVES IT A LOT OF PUNCH," SHE SAYS. "THIS ROOM DOESN'T GET A LOT OF LIGHT, BECAUSE FROM THE BACK, IT'S NORTH LIGHT, AND IN FRONT THERE'S A PORCH."

**LEFT BELOW** THE WHITE AGA STOVE BURNS 24 HOURS A DAY, EVEN IN THE SUMMER. "THE ISLAND IS VERY HUMID IN THE SUMMER," VON UNRUH EXPLAINS. "TO MAINTAIN A CERTAIN DRYNESS IN THE HOUSE, THE AGA EMITS HEAT, WARMS UP THE AIR AND AND CONTAINS THE HUMIDITY." THE STOVE HAS AMPLE OVENS, WHICH THE FAMILY USES FOR ROASTING AND BAKING. AND WHEN THE TEMPERATURE DROPS, AS IT DOES DURING THE SUMMER NIGHTS, THE STOVE IS A PLACE TO LEAN AGAINST WHILE DRINKING A GLASS OF WINE.

**OPPOSITE** VON UNRUH CHOSE TOM DIXON'S CANTILEVERED RUSH CHAIR BECAUSE OF ITS TEXTURE AND ITS SCULPTURAL SHAPE, AND JUXTAPOSED IT WITH A FRENCH WOOD TABLE OF UNKNOWN PROVENANCE. ANOTHER LIGHT TOUCH IS THE WHITE SLIPCOVER FOR THE EASY CHAIR — SHE DESIGNED IT TO TIE IN THE BACK AND FASTEN WITH HORN BUTTONS. IT IS AS IF THE CHAIR WERE CORSETED.

The area of mid-coast Maine where Mallory Marshall and her family summer has no bars, restaurants, or movies, she says. People sew, read and talk and a seasonal highlight is the day the skunk cabbage squeaks. "Maine either rejects you or accepts you," says Marshall, an interior designer. "It doesn't like bland, doesn't like mean, doesn't like coy." It apparently likes her and her husband, Peter Haffenreffer, a retired brewery executive. They own two summer houses, in an estate complete with its own cemetery, and a tiny, two-story Victorian cottage, which is nestled on the narrowest part of an island, so that water is on both sides of the house. It is this little house that Marshall loves the best. The most personal and intimate of the two homes, it has been designed for weekend guests, for friends to write their novels, and for the newly-in-love to hide away in.

# SUMMER STYLE

**OPPOSITE** THIS IS THE GINGERBREAD ENTRANCE TO MARSHALL'S NINETEENTH-CENTURY VICTORIAN COTTAGE IN MAINE. THE HOUSE, AS ROMANTIC INSIDE AS IT IS OUT, IS USED AS A GUEST HOUSE FOR FRIENDS, NEWLYWEDS AND WRITERS IN RETREAT. IT IS PAINTED MOSTLY WHITE, EXCEPT FOR A SOFT GREEN ECHOING THE COLOR OF THE SEA.

**RIGHT** THE HOUSE IS ON THE NARROWEST ROAD ON THE ISLAND, AND IS SURROUNDED BY WATER IN FRONT AND IN BACK. THERE IS A VIEW OF THE WATER FROM NEARLY EVERY WINDOW. THE PORCH FACES EAST, AND HERE MARSHALL HAS COFFEE WITH HER GUESTS EVERY MORNING.

The house is almost entirely white, inside and out. "New England is about looking outdoors," says Marshall. Nature provides emotional resources for people to live by themselves, "so rooms are backdrops for what you're looking at outside". For colors within the house, she chose only those that reflect what is outside, like painted green floors, the same muted shade as the ocean on a cold winter day.

Each room has its own romantic ambience. The screened porch faces east to the water. A second porch is designed for sleeping within glass walls, while a third outdoor porch has been converted into an extra shower, enclosed within plain cedar walls, and open to the sky.

The presence of May Sarton, the writer, hovers over the house. "I just like her," says Marshall. "I used to go and hear her speak, and when she died around five years ago they auctioned all her things." At the auction in Portland, she bought a handkerchief, a tiny memento, while her husband bought her what she really wanted – a portrait of May Sarton, which hangs over the mantel.

The scale of the house is intimate, and Marshall designed it to be gracious. She installed small white wicker gates as a simple entry to the cottage. One of the bathrooms is furnished with a chair that leans back at an angle designed solely for relaxation. "It's if you want to talk to someone who's taking a bath," says Marshall. This is a house that does not demand social ceremony. It invites contemplation, reverie and provides opportunities for simple entertainment.

**LEFT ABOVE** MARSHALL IS ADEPT AT
FINDING ANONYMOUS OBJECTS,
RESTORING THEM, AND UNIFYING THE
DISPARATE PIECES BY PAINTING
OR UPHOLSTERING THEM IN WHITE. THE
ROCKING CHAIR WAS A TREASURE FOUND
ONE DAY AT THE DUMP.
THE CUPBOARD AND TABLE, JUST VISIBLE
BEYOND THE LATTICE DOOR, ARE
TWO MISMATCHED OBJECTS,
ONE PERCHED ON THE OTHER.

**LEFT BELOW** THE SAME MUTED GREEN
OF THE FRONT DOOR IS PRESENT HERE IN
THE SLIPCOVERED CHAIR AND
PILLOWS. THE THEME OF THE ROOM'S
DECOR IS NATURE, EMBODIED BY
THE PINE CONES THAT PARADE ALONG THE
LINTEL ABOVE THE WINDOWS AND
ON THE WRITING TABLE. BOTANICAL
PRINTS HANG ON THE WALLS.

**OPPOSITE** WHEN THE TOP OF
HER ENDTABLE BROKE OFF, MARSHALL
DECIDED TO MAKE CREATING A NEW
ONE A RAINY DAY PROJECT. SHE
COLLECTED HUNDREDS OF PERIWINKLE
SHELLS IN AS MANY COLORS AS SHE
COULD FIND, IN SHADES OF GRAY, PURPLE
AND GREEN, AND GLUED THEM
TO THE TOP OF THE TABLE TO MAKE AN
UNUSUAL SURFACE. ONCE, WHEN
A GROUP OF LITTLE BOYS GATHERED
AROUND HER HOUSE, SHE SUGGESTED THEY
GATHER PERIWINKLES, TOO, AND MAKE
SOMETHING. LATER, THEY
PRESENTED HER WITH A FOUR-FOOT HIGH
OBELISK MADE OF PERIWINKLES.

ABOVE MARSHALL AND
HER INTERIOR DESIGN PARTNER, JAMES
LIGHT, HAVE PAINTED THE STEPS
UP TO THE SECOND FLOOR TO RESEMBLE A
RUNNER, AND ON THE PORCH,
THEY PAINTED THE FLOOR TO RESEMBLE A
HERRINGBONE PATTERNED RUG.

a long love, deepens with time
May Sarton · 19

**LEFT** MARSHALL IS A FAN OF THE WRITER MAY SARTON, AND HAS EMBROIDERED THE COVERLET IN HER BEDROOM WITH A LINE FROM ONE OF HER POEMS: "SOLITUDE, LIKE A LONG LOVE, DEEPENS WITH TIME." RECOGNIZING THAT THE ROMANCE OF HER COTTAGE COULD ENCOURAGE INDOLENCE, MARSHALL HAS HUNG A WIRE BASKET AT THE SIDE OF THE BED, AND WHEN SHE HAS GUESTS SHE FILLS IT WITH CANDY SO THAT WHOEVER IS IN BED CAN LIE THERE ALL DAY WITH CHOCOLATES WITHIN REACH AT ALL TIMES.

**RIGHT ABOVE** AT THE FOOT OF THE BED, MARSHALL HAS CREATED A SMALL TABLEAU. A MARITIME PICTURE TO GAZE AT, A MIRROR RESTING ON A NON-MATCHING BUREAU, AND A CHAIR WITH A RUFFLED PILLOW. IN THIS VICTORIAN COTTAGE, A RUFFLE HERE AND A SWATH OF ORGANDIE THERE DON'T LOOK OUT OF PLACE.

**RIGHT BELOW** A BATH IN THIS ROOM COULD TAKE HOURS. THE TUB IS HIGH ENOUGH, AND THE WINDOW LOW ENOUGH, FOR THE BATHER TO SEE THE OCEAN, AND MARSHALL HAS EVEN ADDED A CHAIR FOR THOSE WHO LIKE COMPANY WHEN BATHING.

The husband found their home, an 1830 English-Dutch-style barn, at a party. He met a newspaperman whose hobby was finding old barns, asked about his biggest one, bought it, and moved it from Manalapan, New Jersey, to Martha's Vineyard, Massachusetts. The barn sits in the reconfigured footprint of a previous barn, which over the years, had deteriorated and was finally torn down.

What delights the couple about their extraordinary summer home is the location. "It's up on the hill overlooking a pond, and overlooking the ocean," says the husband who wishes to remain anonymous. Unusually-shaped windows – some with mullions, some without – frame the views.

The barn is austerely furnished with objects collected over the years, especially chairs dating from the eighteenth century. The stark architecture of the barn stands out, and the spareness and casualness of the furnishings

# THE BIG BARN

appear entirely appropriate and understated for such a rustic home. In the huge, voluminous space, the furniture stands silhouetted, as if each chair, table, and screen were a singular sculptural object. The ambience of the house is quintessential New England style. Little is new. Nothing is flashy. Everything is understated. The home is all about volume, space, strong lines – and almost nothing at all about decor.

The floor of the living area is painted a pale blue-gray, so that the furniture appears to sit lightly on it. In another section of the house, the floorboards are three-inch thick tongue-in-groove yellow pine, recycled from the roofs of knitting mills in the Connecticut Valley.

The dining room is an unusual tableau. The owner made the wood table for a birthday party and topped it with an Oriental runner and a sheet of glass. He then surrounded the long rectangular table with a delightfully motley collection of chairs, dating from the eighteenth century through to the nineteenth. Some chairs are dark wood, some are light-colored wood, and a few are painted white. No two chairs match. He and his wife have seated 32 people around the table, "but generally," he says, "it's about 24."

On a south-facing porch, there is a chair made of woven oak strips. Curved corner chairs face each other in another part of the house and make a cozy, intimate nook, a place to have tea and enjoy the brilliant sun that is filtered through white curtains.

It is said that Leif Eriksson wintered here, but the current family does not, for the winter wind is harsh. This house is a place for summers.

**LEFT ABOVE** THE FAMILY TOOLS AROUND
MARTHA'S VINEYARD IN THEIR
1950 CHRYSLER WINDSOR HIGHLANDER,
WHICH HAS A RED LEATHER
AND TARTAN INTERIOR. THE CAR'S CLASSIC
LINES SEEM TO MELD WITH THE
LANDSCAPE. THE LAND ORIGINALLY
BELONGED TO INDIANS, AND IT IS SAID
THAT IN THE NINETEENTH CENTURY
LEIF ERIKSSON WINTERED HERE.

**LEFT BELOW** ON THE PORCH SITS A
CONVENIENTLY SITUATED STAND FOR
THE WOOD CROQUET MALLETS
THAT OCCASIONALLY GET USED IN THE
SUMMER. THE STAID, PRECISE
ELEGANCE OF THE GAME FITS PERFECTLY
WITH THE GENTEEL WAY OF LIFE
ON THIS LITTLE ISLAND.

**OPPOSITE** THE NINETEENTH-CENTURY BARN
IS ACTUALLY A "BANK BARN",
AS THE OWNER EXPLAINS.
"IF THE WINDOWS WEREN'T THERE,
YOU WOULD BE ABLE TO DRIVE
UNDERNEATH IT, AND ON THE OTHER SIDE
IT'S EIGHT FEET HIGHER."
BUILT ON A BANK, THE BARN IS
SITUATED AMONGST ABUNDANT GREENERY;
LEADING AWAY FROM THE HOUSE IS
A PRIMROSE PATH WHICH EVENTUALLY
WINDS INTO AN OLIVE GROVE.

RIGHT  A PRISTINE WHITE FOSSIL,
THE THREE-FOOT-HIGH SHOULDER BLADE
OF A FIN WHALE, LEANS
AGAINST WHITE-PAINTED STAIRS —
A STUDY OF WHITE ON WHITE. THE BLUE-
PAINTED FLOOR SERVES TO
ACCENTUATE THE PURITY OF THE BONE.

LEFT  THE OWNER BUILT THIS
WOOD TABLE FOR A BIRTHDAY PARTY
AND COVERED IT WITH AN
ORIENTAL RUNNER AND A SHEET OF
GLASS. HE HAS SURROUNDED IT
WITH A DIVERSE COLLECTION OF
EIGHTEENTH- AND NINETEENTH-CENTURY
CHAIRS. THE TABLE HAS
SEATED UP TO 32 PEOPLE FOR DINNER.

OPPOSITE  WHEN THE BARN WAS
RENOVATED, THE BEAMS BECAME A MAJOR
FOCUS FOR ANYONE WALKING INTO
THE VAST, AIRY SPACE. THE OWNERS HAVE
DELINEATED DIFFERENT LIVING
AREAS BY A SEEMINGLY CASUAL PLACEMENT
OF FURNITURE. THE BLUE-GRAY
PAINTED FLOOR DEFINES ONE SECTION OF
THE AREA. A SCREEN MARKS ONE
PERIMETER, AND TO THE RIGHT, BEHIND
THE SCREEN, A FEW CHAIRS
ARE SCATTERED FOR A MORE INTIMATE
ATMOSPHERE. THE FLOOR IN
THE HALLWAY IS NATURAL WOOD
RECYCLED FROM THE
ROOFS OF KNITTING MILLS IN THE
CONNECTICUT VALLEY. CREAMY
COLORED MATERIAL PROVIDES PRIVACY
FOR ONE OF THE ROOMS.

ABOVE  RUBY, A TABBY CAT,
NAPS ON A BLUE-PAINTED WICKER CHAIR
TUCKED INTO A CORNER OF THE
BIG ROOM, CLOSE TO A WINDOW. THE
OCCASIONAL USE OF COLOR, LIKE THE BLUE
ON THE CHAIR, IS A SMALL
PUNCTUATION MARK IN AN OTHERWISE
AUSTERELY FINISHED HOME.
MORE OFTEN SPACE — RATHER THAN
FURNISHINGS — DOMINATE.

RIGHT  AN APPEALING ASPECT OF THIS
TABLEAU IS THE REPEATED
RECTANGULAR SHAPE. THE WHITE SOFA
APPEARS TO FLOAT IN THE MIDDLE
OF THE ROOM, BACKLIT AND FRAMED
BY THE VAST WINDOW.
THE IDEA IS NOT TO FACILITATE AN
INTIMATE GATHERING BUT SIMPLY TO
ACCENTUATE AND ENJOY
THE EXCEPTIONAL SPACIOUSNESS
OF THE BARN. THE EMPTY SPACE AND THE
GENERALLY NEUTRAL COLORS CREATE AN
ATMOSPHERE OF TRANQUILITY.

**BELOW** WHEN THE OWNERS
MOVED THE 50 x 38-FOOT BARN FROM
NEW JERSEY TO MARTHA'S VINEYARD
IN 1979, THEY BUILT ON AN
L-SHAPED ADDITION OF 50 x 25 FEET.
ALTHOUGH IT IS NOW ALMOST
TOO LARGE FOR THEM, THE SITUATION
OF THE BARN ON TOP OF A HILL,
WITH VIEWS OF THE WATER FROM ALMOST
EVERY WINDOW, MEANS THAT THEY
ARE RELUCTANT TO MOVE. THERE ARE
ONLY TWO OTHER HOUSES NEARBY,
SO THE PANORAMIC VIEWS OF
THE LANDSCAPE, THE WATER AND THE
SKY ARE VIRTUALLY UNSPOILED.

This shingle-style house is so beautifully sited that it appears to have been there for a long time, but this is an illusion. In 1991, Lucinda Lang hired architect Jack Valerio to design a house that followed the sun (Lang owns 1,000 acres in a village in Maine and rents summerhouses on her property.) As Lang wakes up each morning, the sun is rising over a bit of the Atlantic Ocean that has edged its way between Mescungus Bay and Penobscot Bay. From her bedroom window, she sees the surf rushing up against the Maine coast with its big, black rocks. In the spring, the water looks turquoise, but darkens in winter.

The kitchen window faces west, so when she makes dinner for herself, her friends and her three dogs, she sees the sunset over the garden. The largest windows of the dining room and sitting room look south, straight towards the water. When the moon is full, the sea is bathed in silver light.

# SIMPLE LIVING

OPPOSITE THE MAIN ENTRANCE FACES NORTH, SO THAT WHEN YOU ENTER, YOU WALK TOWARDS THE WATER, LOOKING SOUTH. LUCINDA LANG, WHO WAS BORN IN NEW ORLEANS, IS A FIRM CONVERT TO NEW ENGLAND STYLE: "I UNDERSTAND THE STYLE AS PRETTY SIMPLE, USING OLD THINGS FROM THE AREA – OLD RATHER THAN NEW," SHE SAYS. THE PADDLE WITH HER NAME INSCRIBED ONTO IT ADDS A TOUCH OF PERSONALITY TO THE PORCH.

RIGHT LANG HAS GROUPED A SET OF WHITE ADIRONDACK CHAIRS FACING THE ATLANTIC OCEAN ON THE FRONT LAWN. SHE AND HER FRIENDS HAVE COOKOUTS THERE DURING THE BRIEF MAINE SUMMER.

Although Lang grew up in New Orleans, she says, "I've been indelibly attracted to New England for my entire life." She loves being on the water, the simple style of living in Maine, of mixing family heirlooms with flea market finds. She finds comfort in objects, whether paintings or pillows, that have been handed down, generation to generation.

In the summer, Lang covers the sitting room sofas with white slipcovers – a classic New England tradition. In winter, she takes them off, leaving the sofas in their original dark green upholstery, and warms the room by lining the windowsills with many pots of plants, turning it into a conservatory. Extravagant linen drapes, pale yellow-green on one side, taupe on the other, flank the room and keep the house warm on cold nights. A low-hanging candelabra hovers over the coffee table, filled with cream-colored tapers ready to be lighted.

In the kitchen mismatched chairs, some from her family, others from yard sales, are grouped around an old marble table, which has been in her family for generations. White pottery, neatly arranged, lines the shelves: mugs on one shelf, pitchers on another. Mixing bowls are in an assortment of shapes and sizes. A child's painting easel and chair stand next to the wood-burning stove.

Throughout the sun-dappled house, there are flowers cut from the garden, which is lavishly planted with purple and blue delphiniums, pink and white cosmos, and red, yellow and orange zinnias. In the garden, white Adirondack chairs face the Atlantic and its wild, wild surf.

LEFT "UNPRETENTIOUSNESS IS KEY IN NEW
ENGLAND," SAYS LANG. IN THIS
ARRANGEMENT OF PICTURES AND OBJECTS,
SHE HAS MIXED FAMILY HAND-ME-DOWNS
WITH THINGS PICKED UP IN YARD SALES
AND TREASURED PHOTOGRAPHS AND
DRAWINGS. THE LAMP WITH THE DOG BASE
IS A FAMILY HEIRLOOM, AND THE FLORAL
IRON PIECES WERE ORIGINALLY DOOR STOPS.

RIGHT SINCE THE HOUSE WAS
DESIGNED TO FOLLOW THE SUN, THE
KITCHEN FACES WEST, AND WHEN
LANG BEGINS TO PREPARE DINNER SHE
CAN WATCH THE SUN SET.
THE OLD MARBLE DINING TABLE IS
ANOTHER FAMILY HEIRLOOM, BROUGHT
FROM NEW ORLEANS. THE CHAIRS
ARE A RANDOM MIX OF UNMATCHED
PIECES, UNIFIED ONLY BY
A THICK COAT OF WHITE PAINT.

OPPOSITE ALTHOUGH IT
DOESN'T TEND TO GET VERY HOT IN THE
SUMMER IN MAINE, LANG ALWAYS
SETS OUT A TABLE AND CHAIRS
IN THE BREEZEWAY TO PROVIDE SOME
RESPITE FROM THE SUN
FOR THOSE WHO NEED IT. SHE AND
HER FRIENDS CAN SIT HERE
AND WATCH THE CROWS, FINCHES
AND BOBOLINKS IN THE FIELD.
DELPHINIUM, ROSA RUGOSA, ZINNIAS AND
COSMOS BLOOM IN THE GARDEN.

ABOVE OUTSIDE, HAWKS AND CROWS CAN BE SEEN SILHOUETTED AGAINST THE SKY, PERCHED ON TREE TOPS. IN THE SITTING ROOM, THIS CARVED WOODEN CROW ACTS AS A REMINDER OF THE BEAUTY OF THE OUTDOORS.

**LEFT** THE SOFA IS DECKED IN ITS SUMMER
FINERY WHILE THE DIFFERENT STYLES
OF FURNITURE ALL ARRANGED TOGETHER
IS ONE OF LANG'S DESIGN
CHARACTERISTICS, KEEPING THE
ROOMS FRESH, INFORMAL AND FRIENDLY.

**RIGHT** THE SITTING ROOM IS FLOODED BY
SUN. IN THE WINTER, LANG TRANSFORMS
THE ROOM INTO A MAKESHIFT
CONSERVATORY, WHEN SHE BRINGS IN
POTS AND POTS OF GERANIUMS. SHE
SHARES HER HOME WITH THREE DOGS
WHO ARE WELCOME EVERYWHERE. THEY
SNOOZE ON THE WHITE SLIPCOVERED
SOFAS IN THE SUMMER, ON THE HOOKED
RUG IN THE KITCHEN, OR THE DOG BED
IN THE MASTER BEDROOM.

Geo. Davis built his home in Nantucket to follow the sun and to focus on the outside. He wanted the sun rising in the kitchen and setting in the sun room. Once he finished the architecture, he painted the background entirely white – there is barely a speck of color in the house. He wants nature to be the focus and to let the light outside color the walls. Colors other than white would have competed with the view and the garden, Davis says, "White lets all the colors come in. The night before last, the sunset was orange and purple, and it colored all the walls, and the French doors, and the window shutters."

Nearly every piece of furniture in the house is wood, and has been stripped down to its natural, often blond color. "I love natural wood without varnish," says Davis, an interior designer and antique dealer, "I like unusual pieces, nineteenth-century English and French pieces, and I like white,

# WHITE ON WHITE

OPPOSITE FROM HIS BED DAVIS CAN LOOK NORTH THROUGH THE GLASS DOORS BEYOND THE PORCH ONTO THE WATER. EVERYTHING IN THE ROOM IS ON A HUGE SCALE, LIKE THE FALCON THAT APPEARS TO SOAR FROM ITS PERCH ON THE WALL – A FIGUREHEAD FROM AN AMERICAN YACHT THAT SANK IN THE MEDITERRANEAN IN THE 1920S. THE 1860S DESK IS MADE OF FAUX BAMBOO.

RIGHT THIS IS A PERFECT EXAMPLE OF DAVIS'S CRAFT. THE STARK FLOOR AND WALLS PROVIDE A NEUTRAL BACKGROUND FOR THE NINETEENTH-CENTURY MARBLE FEMALE TORSO, GENTLY LIT BY THE SUNLIGHT POURING THROUGH THE BLINDS.

white, white." His house, a gray clapboard building built in 1994 in the style of a nineteenth-century farmhouse, mirrors his passions. The interior is completely white, and each room has at least one strong, oversized piece of furniture – a wooden fireplace with a carved surround, a sentry box embellished with a carved wooden deer head – whose provenance is usually French or English and whose wood is usually blond.

The pure white background is a foil for the scupltural pieces of furniture, which he chooses for their big, strong, sculptural lines, idiosyncrasy and embellishment. He is not a mininalist though. Davis loves swooping gestures, extravagant silhouettes, and the eccentric touch of the handcraft. He believes in ornament and decoration.

The guest suite is sybaritic. In the all-white bedroom, an antique bedspread covers the French iron bed, with a new white blanket tossed over for extra warmth. The bathroom repeats his favorite theme: an American pine chest with an oversize pine-framed mirror above, in, of course, a white room.

For guests who like to write, Davis has designed a writer's nook in the hallway adjacent to the bedroom, and painted white the American Victorian wicker and bentwood chair, desk, and table. He took unused space and turned it into a sunny sanctuary, brightened with plants.

In one room he designed a charming window seat that doubles as a spare single bed. It has wainscoting on the walls, storage underneath, and binoculars nearby, for a better view of the spectacular coast.

**LEFT** THE GRAY CLAPBOARD HOUSE IS
BUILT IN THE STYLE OF A
NINETEENTH-CENTURY FARMHOUSE, WITH
ASYMMETRICAL GABLES AND EAVES.
DAVIS CHOSE IT BECAUSE HE LOVED THE
SITE, WITH VIEWS OF WASHING
POND AND NANTUCKET SOUND.
THE WINDSWEPT LANDSCAPE, WHILE A
HOSTILE ENVIRONMENT FOR TALL TREES,
ATTRACTS WILDLIFE SUCH AS EGRETS,
OSPREY, HAWKS, AND OWLS.

**LEFT BOTTOM** THE WHITE PAINTWORK AND
SLEEK BALUSTERS
OFFER A STRIKING CONTRAST
TO THE NATURAL WOOD AND THE
STRONG EQUINE FIGURE
OVERLOOKING THE STAIRCASE.

**OPPOSITE** DAVIS FRAMED THE MUD ROOM
WITH DORIC COLUMNS — A THEATRICAL
GESTURE THAT HAS MADE THIS
HOMELY ROOM SEEM MORE INTRIGUING.
DAVIS LIKES DRAMA AND ORNAMENT;
PLATES PAINTED WITH DOGS HANG
INCONGRUOUSLY ON THE WALL,
WHILE SCUFFED BOOTS AND LOAFERS
ARE LINED UP NEATLY ON THE
FLOOR, AND SPARE SLICKERS AND
CAPS HANG ON PEGS.

**LEFT** THE SUN STREAMS INTO THE LIVING
ROOM, HIGHLIGHTING THE SET
OF FRENCH LOUVERS ON THE BACK WALL.
THE LOUVERS HAVE NO FUNCTION:
DAVIS INSTALLED THEM PURELY AS A
DECORATIVE GESTURE. HE ALSO RECYCLED
HALF A CANOE TO SERVE AS A
BOOKCASE, ANOTHER OVERSCALED OBJECT
THAT DRAWS THE EYE UPWARD.
THE CANDLESTICK NEAR THE WINDOW IS
EIGHTEENTH-CENTURY ITALIAN
AND WAS ORIGINALLY USED IN A CHURCH.
THE HOUSE IS UNLIKE MOST OTHER
NEW ENGLAND HOMES – "I DON'T
SLIPCOVER THE SOFAS," DAVIS SAYS,
REFERRING TO THE HABIT OF PUTTING WHITE
SLIPCOVERS ON SOFAS IN THE SUMMER AND
TAKING THEM OFF TO REVEAL RUBY
VELVET, FOR EXAMPLE, IN THE WINTER.
"WHITE REMINDS OF ME OF WARM THINGS.
I DON'T RELATE WHITE TO SNOW."

**RIGHT** WHETHER LOOKING OUTWARDS OR
IN, DAVIS LIKES TO FRAME
HIS VIEWS. EVEN FROM THE UPSTAIRS
LANDING, THERE ARE COZY DOMESTIC
VIEWS OF DOWNSTAIRS.
ONE IS OF THE READING NOOK WHICH
IS OFF THE DINING AREA, AN IRRESISTIBLE
INVITATION EVEN TO ACTIVE-NATURED
PEOPLE TO SPEND SOME TIME THERE.
AN ENGLISH WHEELBARROW
ORIGINALLY DESIGNED FOR A CHILD
PROVIDES AN UNUSUAL RECEPTACLE FOR
BOOKS AND MAGAZINES.
SINCE THE CHAIR IS PLACED NEAR THE
FIREPLACE, WITH A BASKET OF
LOGS AND KINDLING NEARBY,
THERE IS THE EXTRA TEMPTATION OF
A BLAZING FIRE ON A COLD WINTER NIGHT.

**LEFT** THE LIGHT-FILLED KITCHEN FACES EAST, SO THAT DAVIS CAN MAKE HIS MORNING COFFEE IN THE LIGHT OF THE BRILLIANT MORNING SUN. THE PRISTINE WHITE KITCHEN IS COMMODIOUS ENOUGH TO HAVE STOOLS AND AN ARMCHAIR SURROUNDING A HANDY ISLAND FOR FRIENDS TO KIBITZ WHILE HE CHOPS THE VEGETABLES FOR A HOMESTYLE DINNER. THE NATURAL COLORS OF THE FLOWERS, FRUIT, AND VEGETABLES LEAP OUT FROM THE PURE BACKGROUND. ALTHOUGH ALL THE FIXTURES AND FITTINGS ARE PAINTED AN UNRELIEVED WHITE, THERE IS NO SHORTAGE OF DIFFERENT TEXTURES AND STYLES.

**OPPOSITE** THE FURNITURE IN DAVIS'S DINING ROOM, A MELANGE OF FRENCH, ENGLISH, AND AMERICAN ANTIQUES, IS MISMATCHED BUT RELATED. EACH BLOND OBJECT HAS BEEN CARVED OR EMBELLISHED IN A BOLD WAY. THE FRENCH PINE FIREPLACE HAS AN ORNATE, CARVED SURROUND AND AN OVAL MIRROR. THE FRENCH-STYLE CHAIRS, WHICH WERE ACTUALLY CARVED IN SPAIN, HAVE OVAL CANED BACKS. NOW AND THEN AN AMERICAN ANTIQUE APPEARS, FOR EXAMPLE, AN UMBRELLA STAND MADE FROM A TREE TRUNK AND WOUND ROUND WITH VINES. THE WHITE FLOWERS, STANDING IN A WOODEN BUCKET, ARE A FURTHER REMINDER OF NATURE.

**RIGHT** IN THE HALLWAY LEADING TO THE GUEST ROOM, DAVIS HAS CREATED A TABLEAU AS AN ODE TO THE FEMALE FORM ON TOP OF AN ENGLISH MACHINIST'S TABLE. A MINIATURE DRESS FORM IS JUXTAPOSED WITH A FRENCH STIRRUP CUP IN THE SHAPE OF A WOMAN'S SHOE. THE MIRROR BEHIND MAKES THE LITTLE CORNER SEEM LARGER AND BRIGHTER, AND THE REFLECTION OF THE TABLEAU ADDS FOCUS.

ABOVE  A SOMEWHAT BATTERED LOOKING
WOODEN HORSE STANDS IN A
CORNER OF THE BEDROOM. DAVIS BOUGHT
IT IN MAINE AND ALTHOUGH
HE DOESN'T KNOW ITS ORIGIN, HE DOES
KNOW THAT IT USED TO BE OF
A MORE NOBLE APPEARANCE.
"IT ONCE HAD LEATHER EARS, AND A
COARSE FIBER MANE," HE SAYS.

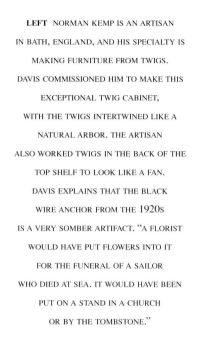

**LEFT** NORMAN KEMP IS AN ARTISAN
IN BATH, ENGLAND, AND HIS SPECIALTY IS
MAKING FURNITURE FROM TWIGS.
DAVIS COMMISSIONED HIM TO MAKE THIS
EXCEPTIONAL TWIG CABINET,
WITH THE TWIGS INTERTWINED LIKE A
NATURAL ARBOR. THE ARTISAN
ALSO WORKED TWIGS IN THE BACK OF THE
TOP SHELF TO LOOK LIKE A FAN.
DAVIS EXPLAINS THAT THE BLACK
WIRE ANCHOR FROM THE 1920S
IS A VERY SOMBER ARTIFACT. "A FLORIST
WOULD HAVE PUT FLOWERS INTO IT
FOR THE FUNERAL OF A SAILOR
WHO DIED AT SEA. IT WOULD HAVE BEEN
PUT ON A STAND IN A CHURCH
OR BY THE TOMBSTONE."

**RIGHT ABOVE** TWIG FURNITURE IN A
VERNACULAR STYLE FURNISHES
A BATHROOM. SINCE TWIG CHAIRS AREN'T
PARTICULARLY COMFORTABLE TO
SIT ON, DAVIS HAS PLACED A PILLOW ON
THE SLATTED SEAT. A BARK
WASTE BASKET IS A PERFECT COMPLEMENT
TO THE TWIG TABLE AND CHAIR.

**RIGHT BELOW** THE WIRE SCULPTURE
OF A FISH SUSPENDED FROM
THE SLOPING CEILING EMPHASIZES THE
MARITIME THEME IN THIS SPACE:
ON TOP OF THE FRENCH CONSOLE DAVIS
HAS CREATED A TINY SEASIDE
SETTING WITH AN ENGLISH DIORAMA
OF A SHIP, AN ANCHOR, AND SOME
SEASHELLS TO COMPLETE THE IMAGE.

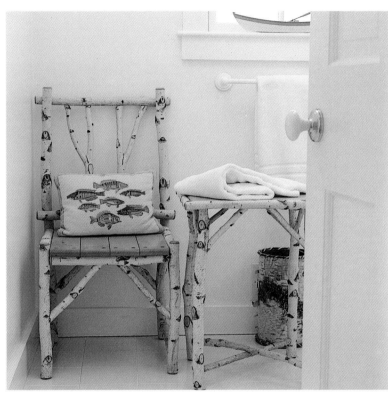

in the
WILD

Ross Anderson, a Manhattan architect, his wife, Nina Santisi, a film producer, and their daughter, Eva, live in what he calls, tongue-in-cheek, "The Hovel." In more grandiose moments, he calls their 650-square-foot weekend house, a "summerhaus," which they built with the help of friends. In Manhattan, Anderson designs residences and offices, especially for the new wave of internet-based businesses. The common characteristic of these companies is flux – continual upgrading of computers and software and the rapid turnaround of personnel. In Dummerston, Vermont, however, Anderson has designed a simple retreat for his family, based on a tobacco barn. "It's a woven basket that contains a screen porch and loft, dog trot/mud room, and a winterized portion that has a kid's room and living quarters," says Anderson. By any name, it is a simple yet highly inventive home that sits quietly amid 100 acres of land,

# THE WOVEN BASKET

**OPPOSITE** THE SMALL HOUSE NESTLES UNOBTRUSIVELY AMONG 100 ACRES OF ROLLING LANDSCAPE. IT HAS BEEN PAINTED A SUBTLE BLACK SO THAT IT DISAPPEARS INTO THE BACKGROUND RATHER THAN DRAWING ATTENTION AWAY FROM THE VIEW. THE WHITE-PAINTED PART IS THE NON-WINTERIZED SLEEPING PORCH, A PLACE INHABITED ONLY DURING THE SUMMER.

**RIGHT** IN HOT WEATHER, ANDERSON OPENS THE SLIDING DOORS, SO THAT THE ENTIRE HOUSE BECOMES A BREEZEWAY. THE DINING AREA IS TYPICALLY INFORMAL, THE TABLE A PIECE OF JUNK SURROUNDED BY CLASSIC CHAIRS, EITHER BY THONET OR CHARLES EAMES.

nearly disappearing into the luxuriant Vermont landscape. It's a cross between a Connecticut River Valley tobacco barn and a house. "I wanted to bridge the line between a domestic building and an agricultural one," Anderson says. "I didn't want to it look like a barn or a cute little house."

Tobacco barns have adjustable shutters to control the temperature and ensure the tobacco dries properly. Anderson translated the shutters into floor-to-ceiling sliding doors on both sides of the house to control the temperature, and when the doors are open, the entire house becomes a breezeway. He designed some of the walls as horizontal wood slats alternating with fiberglass strips, so that the house is partly translucent. "At night it glows softly like a paper lantern in the woods," he says.

"The classic house in Vermont is white clapboard, with horizontal slats," the architect says, who stained the pine boards of the winterized part of the house black, but painted the porch white. "The black allows the landscape to stand out against the maples, birch, and ash trees."

After the couple bought the land in 1989, they had a road constructed, cleared the meadows, put in the pond and the wood-fired hot tub, and began building the house. They built the jutting platform in 1992, and the house during the next two years, with the winterized part (kitchen and living quarters) on the platform, and the screened-in sleeping porch in the rear, nestled into a moss-covered rock ledge. Someday the house will have a proper bathroom, barn and sauna (at the moment there are only the basics – a bathtub, and an outhouse).

LEFT HOUSES LARGER THAN 6,500 SQUARE
FEET HAVE THEIR OWN MUD ROOMS FOR
WINTER COATS AND BOOTS. THIS HOUSE IS
SO SMALL THAT THERE IS ONLY ROOM FOR A
MUD CORNER. THE OARS LEANING UP
AGAINST THE FUNCTIONAL WOODEN BENCH
ILLUSTRATE THE LARGELY OUTDOOR LIFE
ENJOYED BY THE WHOLE FAMILY.

LEFT BELOW ALTHOUGH THIS TINY HOME
HAS AN OUTHOUSE AND NO FLUSH TOILET,
TWO MIRRORS ALLOW FOR A TOUCH
OF COMFORT AND EVEN
VANITY – AND WASHING FACILITIES,
WHILE PRIMITIVE, ARE CERTAINLY STYLISH.

RIGHT ANDERSON BUILT WALLS MADE
OF HORIZONTAL WOOD SLATS,
SO THAT THE WIND BLOWS INTO THE
ROOM, AND EVEN AROUND
THE WINDOWS. THE WALLS ARE
PARTLY TRANSLUCENT. LIGHT FALLS IN
STRIPES ONTO THE FLOOR
AND THE OAK CHAIR DESIGNED
BY THE ARCHITECT.
ANDERSON CALLS IT A MODERN VERSION
OF THE ADIRONDACK CHAIR.
HE HAS TOSSED A WHITE SHEEPSKIN OVER
THE SWIVEL CHAIR, ADDING TO
THE COZY ATMOSPHERE. ANDERSON
EXPLAINS THAT HE FEELS
AS IF HE IS SITTING IN A WOVEN BASKET
WHEN HE IS IN THIS ROOM.
AND AT NIGHT, WHEN THEY LIGHT THE
CANDLES AND KEROSENE LAMPS,
THE HOUSE GLOWS FROM WITHIN.
THE WALLS AND FLOOR ARE MADE FROM
LOCAL PINE. "IT'S CHEAP AND SIMPLE,"
SAYS ANDERSON. "YOU JUST
CALL UP THE LOCAL GUY."

138

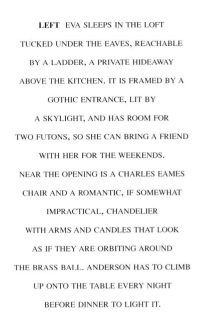

**LEFT** EVA SLEEPS IN THE LOFT TUCKED UNDER THE EAVES, REACHABLE BY A LADDER, A PRIVATE HIDEAWAY ABOVE THE KITCHEN. IT IS FRAMED BY A GOTHIC ENTRANCE, LIT BY A SKYLIGHT, AND HAS ROOM FOR TWO FUTONS, SO SHE CAN BRING A FRIEND WITH HER FOR THE WEEKENDS. NEAR THE OPENING IS A CHARLES EAMES CHAIR AND A ROMANTIC, IF SOMEWHAT IMPRACTICAL, CHANDELIER WITH ARMS AND CANDLES THAT LOOK AS IF THEY ARE ORBITING AROUND THE BRASS BALL. ANDERSON HAS TO CLIMB UP ONTO THE TABLE EVERY NIGHT BEFORE DINNER TO LIGHT IT.

**RIGHT** THE KITCEN AND DINING AREA ARE DIRECTLY BELOW EVA'S SLEEPING LOFT. THE DINING TABLE IS SURROUNDED BY MARCEL BREUER'S BENTWOOD CHAIRS, STAINED CELADON. THE CABINETS ARE BIRCH, AND THE FOUR-BURNER WHITE ENAMEL GAS STOVE, WHICH DATES FROM THE TURN OF THE CENTURY, STILL WORKS.

**LEFT** A STUDY OF METAL UPON METAL. A WIRE BASKET HOLDS A PAIR OF CAST BRASS BABIES' HEADS, WHICH HAVE BECOME BATTERED AND COLORED GREEN WITH TIME. THEIR WORN PATINAS AND HOLLOWED FACES GIVE THEM A GHOULISH APPEARANCE. ALTHOUGH THEY ARE ACTUALLY MADE OF SOLID BRASS, THE EFFECT OF OXIDIZATION AGAINST THE ORIGINAL BLACK BACKGROUND MAKES THEM LOOK SOMEHOW VERY SKELETAL.

**LEFT BELOW** A SIMPLE TABLEAU OF PICTURE FRAMES ACTS AS AN UNUSUAL VISUAL STIMULANT. THE RED CROSS WAS A GIFT FROM TIBOR KALMAN, THE GRAPHIC DESIGNER WHO WORKED ON A CONTROVERSIAL MAGAZINE CALLED *COLORS* FOR BENETTON, WHICH FOCUSED ON SUBJECTS LIKE AIDS.

**BELOW** THE HIGH-MAINTENANCE WOOD-BURNING STOVE IS THE SOLE SOURCE OF HEAT FOR THE LITTLE HOUSE. IN WINTER, IT CAN BE SO COLD THAT THE FAMILY CAN SEE THEIR OWN BREATH. HOWEVER, ADORNED WITH PILES OF SMOOTH PEBBLES AND HAND-THROWN VASES, THE STOVE CAN ALSO BECOME A DECORATIVE FEATURE.

**OPPOSITE** SUNSHINE AND THE NEARBY STOVE HEAT THE SLEEPING AREA, A DOUBLE SLEIGH BED WITH BOOKCASES AT BOTH ENDS. STRIPES OF LIGHT FILTER ONTO THE BED AND THE PINE FLOORS. SHEEPSKIN THROWS ADD COZINESS AND TEXTURE TO THE CHAIRS. THERE IS NO NEED FOR CURTAINS IN THIS ISOLATED AREA.

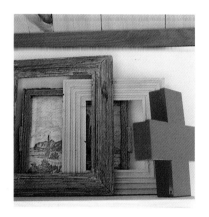

**ABOVE** THIS CARTOON-LIKE SPOTTED PAINTED WOOD DUCK DECOY DATES FROM THE 1960s, AND IT IS PLACED AT THE FOOT OF THE SLEIGH BED, BASKING IN THE SUN. ITS MAIN CHARM IS THAT IT ISN'T VERY REALISTIC, THUS PROBABLY RENDERING IT FAIRLY USELESS AS A WORKING DECOY.

In 1991, John and Carolyn Grace gave up their lives as lawyers in Boston to set up The Atlantic Blanket Company on Swans Island, Maine. Six miles off the shore of Acadia National Park, on an island with a population of 350, the Graces have set up a local industry, hand-dyeing and weaving pure wool blankets.

They divide their time between a big winterized house, which they built in 1993 to accommodate their looms, and a tiny 1,000-square-foot former schoolhouse, which dates from the mid-nineteenth century. The schoolhouse is plain gray clapboard and was moved to the present site, where an extension was added. Heated only by the wood-burning stove in the kitchen, it is more a summerhouse than permanent home, but the Graces spent the winter of 1993 there while the big house was being built, using the stove both for heat and for cooking.

# COTTAGE INDUSTRY

OPPOSITE THE GRACES' HAND-DYED, HAND-WOVEN WOOL BLANKETS ARE OFTEN THE MAJOR FOCAL POINT OF A ROOM, AS IN THE SECOND-FLOOR BEDROOM. THE BLANKETS ARE GRAPHICALLY STRONG, CLEAN LINED, AND BEAUTIFULLY COLORED. THE BLUE IN THE BLANKET IS FROM DYE MADE OF POWDERED INDIGO. THE BED IS A PAINTED WOOD CAMP BED THAT FOLDS UP, AND THE VIEW IS OF MACKEREL COVE.

RIGHT THE MIDNIGHT BLUE COLOR OF THIS OCEAN-SMOOTHED PEBBLE COMPLEMENTS THE INDIGO IN THE SUMMERWEIGHT BLANKET. THE GRACES USE ONLY NATURAL DYES.

When the big house was finished, the Graces wondered what to do with the schoolhouse. "We didn't want to change it," Carolyn says, "We didn't want to winterize it." So they eventually left it exactly as it is – a summerhouse – and wander between the big house and the little one according to the seasons. The bedrooms in the summerhouse are still reserved for their four grown children, who come often for a visit.

A tiny flock of 11 Corriedale sheep graze the land and provide a small part of the wool required to weave the blankets. The rest is chosen from the wool fleece from Maine's Shetland, Columbia, and Corriedale sheep. A spinnery on the island turns the wool into yarn, and the Graces, along with local weavers, produce the blankets by hand on shuttle looms. When the blankets are finished, the edges are carefully bound in silk. The natural colors of the blankets range from misty gray to off-white, dark brown and black, but they are usually hand-dyed using natural pigments of teal green, indigo, and primrose pink. Carolyn makes the dyes herself, using madder root, osage shavings, cochineal shells, and powdered indigo.

The blankets themselves are an essential part of the Graces' home, lending warmth, graphic strength, and tactility to a very old and simple house. Much like the Amish quilts of nineteenth-century Pennsylvania, they are not only examples of fine craftwork, but also strong visual centerpieces. Woven in big checks, plaids, and stripes, the blankets can dominate a room, and along with flowers, friends' paintings, and daughter Claire's ceramic pots, make simple, but nevertheless beautiful adornments.

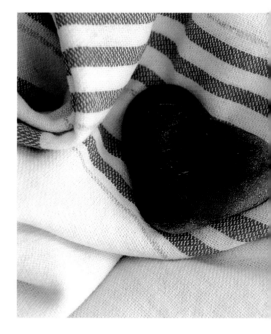

**LEFT ABOVE** THE NINETEENTH-CENTURY CLAPBOARD SHINGLE HOUSE WAS BUILT AROUND 1850 AND WAS ORIGINALLY A SCHOOLHOUSE ON SWANS ISLAND. IT WAS MOVED SOMETIME IN THE EARLY TWENTIETH CENTURY TO THE PRESENT SITE AND ADDED ON. THE GRACES BUILT A WINTER HOUSE BEHIND THE SUMMER HOUSE IN 1993 AND THEY SPEND THE COLDEST MONTHS OF THE YEAR THERE.

**LEFT BELOW** THE WOOL FROM THE GRACES' 11 CORRIEDALE SHEEP PROVIDES ONLY A SMALL PORTION OF THAT NEEDED FOR THE FAMILY'S LOCAL, HANDS-ON INDUSTRY.

**RIGHT** THE GRACES LIVE A RUGGED LIFE, BEARING WITH THE BITTER COLD, SNOW, AND GUSTING WINDS OF THE MAINE WINTER, AND THE ISOLATION OF AN ISLAND. ALTHOUGH THEY DO HAVE ELECTRICITY, THE WOOD-BURNING STOVE IS THE ONLY SOURCE OF HEAT. FROM 1993 TO 1994, WHILE THEY WERE BUILDING THE WINTERIZED HOUSE, THEY SPENT A LOT OF TIME IN THE KITCHEN HUDDLED AROUND THE STOVE. THE KITCHEN IS ALMOST PRIMITIVE IN ITS SIMPLICITY. THE FLAPS OF THE WOODEN BAKER'S TABLE FOLD OUT TO ACCOMMODATE THE GRACES' FOUR CHILDREN, WHO VISIT IN THE SUMMER.

**ABOVE** SOME FAMILIES WOULD CALL
THIS AREA — HOME FOR SPARE
SLICKERS AND GARDEN BOOTS — A MUD
ROOM. THE GRACES DO NOT.
"WE CALL IT THE BACK SHED,"
CAROLYN GRACE SAYS. THERE IS ORDER
IN THE CLOSET, BUT IT DOESN'T
LOOK FORCED OR ARTIFICIAL.

**BELOW** FROM THE DOWNSTAIRS BEDROOM
THERE IS A PANORAMIC VIEW
OF TOOTHACRE COVE. THE ROOM IS
FURNISHED SIMPLY, WITH
AN ALMOST OFF-HAND USE OF COLOR.
THE WALLS ARE SLATE BLUE,
PART OF THE SAME GENTLE PALETTE
THAT SHOWS UP IN THE BLANKETS.
THE BROWN AND WHITE BLANKET IS
UNSURPRISINGLY MADE OF
NATURAL, UNDYED WOOL. CURTAINS
ARE CASUAL AND MINIMAL,
DRAWING THE EYE TO THE MORE
DRAMATIC COLORS OF THE OUTDOORS.

**LEFT ABOVE** IN THE HALLWAY THE GRACES
HAVE INSERTED COLOR WITH A SURE
BUT SPARING HAND. THEY PAINTED THE TOP
OF THE RISERS AND THE FLOOR IN A
SLATE GRAY, AND PLACED THE EIGHTEENTH-
CENTURY CHAIR FROM JOHN GRACE'S
FAMILY ON A BEAUTIFUL HANDWOVEN RUG.

**LEFT BELOW** ALTHOUGH THE GRACES
LEAD A SIMPLE RURAL LIFE, THEY
WEAVE BLANKETS WITH A CLARITY AND
SUBTLE SOPHISTICATION. THESE PIECES HAVE
THE CLASSIC GRAPHIC DESIGN OF OTHER
TRADITIONAL AMERICAN BLANKETS.

**OPPOSITE** IN THE KITCHEN
ARE PLACED FAMILY HEIRLOOMS OF
A SENTIMENTAL RATHER THAN
A MATERIAL VALUE AS WELL AS ART
CREATED BY FRIENDS.
THE LARGE CHAIR FACING THE DOOR,
FOR EXAMPLE, IS OF NO SPECIAL
PROVENANCE, AS CAROLYN GRACE
EXPLAINS, "IT'S JUST AN OLD CHAIR
FROM JOHN'S FAMILY — MAYBE A
PLANTATION CHAIR OR A STEAMER
CHAIR." THE HAZY PAINTING
IS OF CAPE COD, AND IT WAS CREATED
BY A FAMILY FRIEND.
THE BLUE VASE WAS MADE BY
CLAIRE GRACE, ONE OF
THE FOUR DAUGHTERS OF THE FAMILY,
WHO NUMBERS POTTERY
AMONG HER ACCOMPLISHMENTS.
A FEW ALDERBERRY BRANCHES HELP
TO ESTABLISH A LINK WITH
THE OUTSIDE WORLD.

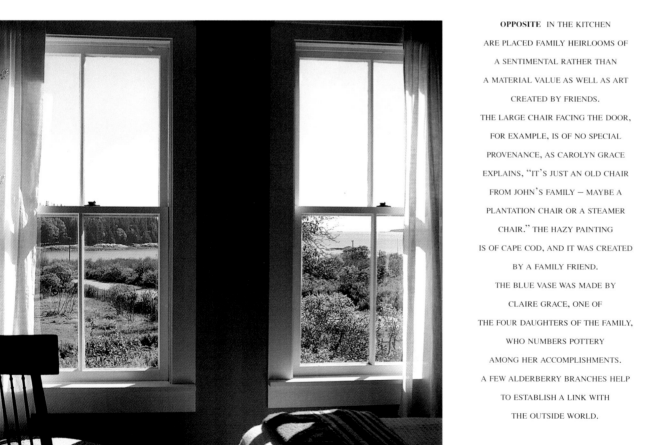

If New England has its own Colonial traditions, Richard Lee, an antique dealer and artist, has created his own mythology. His art consists of surrealistic imagery painted on glass. His work depicts cherubs with roses sprouting from their heads, maidens playing catch with strawberries, and Hindu deities with enlarged phalluses. "I work on a fantastical level," he says. "As over the top as I can. Some see Persian, some see Chinese, some see Bosch. For years, I told people Bosch was my grandfather."

Lee is not a newcomer to Martha's Vineyard. He arrived in 1976 and seldom visits either the mainland or Nantucket. With Simon Hickman, he owns an arts and furniture gallery called Chicamoo, an Algonquin term that comes from the creek where herring once ran on their way to the Atlantic ocean. Chicamoo sells ornately carved, nineteenth-century Victorian furniture, relics found in nearby attics and garages. "If you live

# ECLECTIC ART

OPPOSITE LEE FOUND THE CONSOLE THAT NOW STANDS IN THE ENTRY INTACT BUT BORING, SO HE FAUX MARBLED THE TOP. ABOVE IT HANG A PAIR OF LATE EIGHTEENTH-CENTURY SILHOUETTE PICTURES, WITH THE SILHOUETTES PAINTED ON THE GLASS. "THEY WERE MAIL ORDER KITS," SAYS LEE. "THEY SENT YOU THE BACKGROUND, THE STENCILS FOR THE FIGURES, THE FRAME, AND THE GLASS. YOU DID YOUR OWN STENCILING."

RIGHT LEE ADDED GILDING TO THE NINETEENTH-CENTURY CARVED WOODEN CHAIR TO ADD SOME INTEREST. NEXT TO IT IS ONE OF HIS REVERSE PAINTINGS ON GLASS.

on an island, you never throw anything away," he says. When they buy the furniture, Hickman restores it, and then Lee paints it, often subduing his predilection for all things bright and painting traditional trompe l'oeils, like faux marble.

Lee shares a cedar saltbox in Martha's Vineyard with his wife, Claudia, who designs jewelry, and their son, Hudson. The house is the exact opposite of New England austere. It glitters. It's theatrical. It's electric and eclectic. His glass paintings hang on walls, and fronts of armoires and cupboards. To add to the atmosphere, flickering candle light is caught and multiplied in the glass surfaces. Though now a painter and restorer, Lee used to be a dancer, and in a way this artistic grace has never left him. There is an exuberance to his art that can also be seen in his movements as he leaps about the house barefoot and he says of himself, "I'm too old to be a hippy. I'm a beatnik."

The house is an archive of his work. "I think of it as my workshop," he says. Nearly every piece of furniture bears his mark, whether it's a trompe l'oeil finish, découpage or glass painting. In his studio, he has a sideboard, the legs of which he has cut off and then découpaged with butterflies and birds taken from a calendar from the Metropolitan Museum of Art. There is also a Victorian wood firescreen that he has given a faux marble finish and a screen découpaged with a collection of global images: an Indonesian cigarette advertizement, a carved crystal skull, an Oceanic tribal mask, full of imagery and inspiration from both East and West.

**LEFT ABOVE** LEE FOUND THE
SALVAGED NINETEENTH-CENTURY
MADONNA THAT ONCE ADORNED A
CHURCH IN AN ANTIQUE SHOP.
SHE HAS GLASS EYES.

**LEFT BELOW** A COLLECTION
OF TRIBAL OBJECTS ADORNS THIS
CORNER OF THE ROOM,
ANOTHER ECLECTIC AND EXUBERANT
PART OF LEE'S COLLECTION.

**OPPOSITE** LEE LIKES TO RECYCLE
WHATEVER OBJECTS HE FINDS
ON THE ISLAND, INCLUDING TREE
TRUNKS. A HURRICANE BLEW DOWN
LOCUST TREES ALL OVER
MARTHA'S VINEYARD IN AROUND
1990, AND HE TRANSFORMED
A FEW INTO COLUMNS
FOR HIS STUDIO AFTER THE WOOD
HAD BEEN STRIPPED,
SANDED, AND BUFFED. MOST OF
LEE'S VICTORIAN FURNITURE WAS
FOUND ON THE ISLAND,
STORED IN BARNS AND GARAGES,
SOLD AT TAG SALES,
AND THEN RESTORED BY ARTISTS
LIKE LEE HIMSELF AND SIMON HICKMAN,
HIS PARTNER AT THE
ANTIQUES STORE CHICAMOO. THE MASKS
HANGING ON THE WALL
NEAR THE WINDOW ARE RELICS
FROM HIS HECTIC DAYS
IN MANHATTAN, BEFORE HE MOVED
TO THE VINEYARD, WHEN HE HAD
A MASK SHOP CALLED "LET'S FACE IT."
THE PAINTED MIRROR NEAR
THE DESK DEPICTS A BOY FISHING AND
DATES FROM THE EARLY 1800s.

ABOVE "GLASS PAINTING BEGAN IN
CENTRAL WESTERN EUROPE, IN GERMANY
AND CZECHOSLOVAKIA, AND
PEAKED IN EUROPE IN THE NINETEENTH
CENTURY," LEE EXPLAINS. "PEOPLE HUNG
GLASS PAINTINGS UP HIGH TO
REFLECT LIGHT." IN HIS STUDIO, LEE KEEPS
ALL THE TOOLS REQUIRED TO
PRACTICE THIS ALMOST-FORGOTTEN ART.

**LEFT** SOME OF LEE'S REVERSE
PAINTING ADORN THE GLASS
ON THIS TURN-OF-THE-CENTURY
OAK CHINA CABINET.

**OPPOSITE** LEE EXPLAINS THAT HE
PAINTS AN ECLECTIC
HIERARCHY OF FIGURES, SOME
MYTHOLOGICAL, SOME
RELIGIOUS, SOME FROM THE EAST,
SOME FROM THE WEST.
THIS GROUPING OF OBJECTS NEAR
THE KITCHEN REVEALS HIS
PENCHANT FOR COLLECTING EXOTIC,
GLITTERY THINGS, WHICH HE
TRANSFORMS INTO ART
THAT HE PURPOSEFULLY MAKES "OVER
THE TOP." THE GIRONDELLE,
OR CRYSTAL CANDELABRA, GLITTERS
IN THE SIMPLE SALTBOX KITCHEN.
THE ANGEL-WINGED FOLK ART PIECE IS
TWENTIETH CENTURY, AND
IS ONE OF THE ODD PIECES THAT HE
BOUGHT "OFF-ISLAND" AS
NATIVES OF THE VINEYARD SAY,
SOMEWHERE IN MASSACHUSETTS.
HIGH ON THE ARMOIRE
IS A CARVED WOOD MOLD FROM THE
PHILIPPINES. IT DEPICTS
A CHRISTMAS-CAROLER AND WAS
ORIGINALLY USED
TO MAKE PAPIER-MACHÉ.

The first English settlers began arriving in Nantucket in 1659, and by the eighteenth century it was one of the great whaling centers, not just of the United States, but of the world. Nantucket is an island of history, and interior designer Eugenie Voorhees has become a devout preservationist. In 1998, she ran for election to the Nantucket Historic Districts Commission, which has an elected board of five, and in 1999, she became chair, only to resign in spring of 2000. But she continues to work to keep this Quaker town, full of weathered gray saltboxes and Greek Revival homes, safe from trophy homes, or what she calls "the sprawl." Voorhees says, "People are overbuilding and I'm fighting against the new money that's trying to turn a simple Quaker-inspired saltbox into something it never was." Some of the new buyers preserve the exterior and gut the inside. She does not approve. "It's an educational thing. Most

# LINEAR SIMPLICITY

OPPOSITE EUGENIE VOORHEES'S HOUSE

IS AS PLAIN AS PLAIN CAN

BE – AND ENDEARING IN ITS SIMPLICITY.

THE HINGED DOOR HAS HANDMADE

LATCHES, A LAMP TO TURN

ON AT NIGHT, AND A WINDOW TO PEEK

THROUGH AND TO LET LIGHT IN.

IT SUGGESTS CASUAL FRIENDLINESS,

WITH THE POSSIBILITY OF

KNOCKING AND THEN LIFTING THE

LATCH AND STICKING YOUR HEAD INSIDE

IF THERE IS NO ANSWER.


RIGHT A SHIP'S PORTHOLE, PROVENANCE

UNKNOWN, WAS FITTED INTO THE

OUTSIDE DOOR, A REMINDER

OF NANTUCKET'S SEAFARING HISTORY.

people don't seem to understand that by tearing out the guts of a building and rebuilding it, you destroy the original. What's left is a replica." Vorhees nominated Nantucket to the list of the National Trust for Historic Preservation, and hopes it will make the final list of the 11 most endangered sites in the United States.

On Nantucket, she rents a vernacular 1940s gray clapboard house. A mere thousand square feet in size, it is divided into two stories and is proof that a minimally decorated home can be warm and inviting. "New England is not about show," she says. The house is somewhat dark. So is the woodwork, which includes pine cabinetry and cypress walls. So to brighten the interior, she has covered all the furniture – loveseat, conservatory chairs, beds – in white. Vorhees, who worked for 10 years with David Easton, the Manhattan interior designer, likes white, a color that she finds enormously comforting. To prevent the house from looking too spartan, Vorhees deftly arranges pictures, topiaries, and bayberry branches cut from her garden, where the trees are stunted and the rose hips are hardy enough to survive the endless winds. "Martha's Vineyard has stately elms, Nantucket has scrub oak."

The rented cottage is not luxurious. But it epitomizes a kind of simple yet gracious way of New England living. There is nothing fancy, but neither is any element of home absent. "When you're on an island or in a beach environment," she says, "you should base your design on basic elements and good clean lines." This linear simplicity is her trademark.

**LEFT ABOVE AND BELOW** VOORHEES LIVES
A MINIMAL LIFE IN THIS PLAIN
COTTAGE. SHE HAS ALL THE AMENITIES
OF HOME, BUT FEW
EXTRAS. THOSE ARE DISPLAYED IN
THE SIMPLEST MANNER.
IN THE KITCHEN POTS AND PANS LINE
THE SHELVES ABOVE THE STOVE,
AND TO THE RIGHT HANG TWO
OF HER COLLECTIONS: A CASUAL MIX OF
1820S ADAMS POTTERY,
THE PLATES DECORATED WITH BRIGHT
GREEN FOLIAGE, INTERSPERSED WITH
NEW, WHITE ENAMELWARE.

**OPPOSITE** VORHEES FINDS WHITE THE
MOST COMFORTING COLOR,
AND IN HER PARED-DOWN, GRACIOUS
LIVING ROOM, SHE CAN WATCH
THE WHITE UPHOLSTERY ON THE LOVESEAT
AND CONSERVATORY CHAIRS TAKE ON
DIFFERENT HUES ACCORDING TO
THE DIFFERENT SEASONS. AT NIGHT, WHEN
THE HALOGEN LIGHT IS ON,
THE FABRIC GLOWS SNOW WHITE. ON A
CLOUDY, WINDY DAY, THE FURNITURE TAKES
ON A PALE GRAY CAST. SHE
ADDS COLOR TO THE ROOM BY ADDING
INTERESTING TEXTURES.
A HANDWOVEN THROW FROM NANTUCKET
LOOMS IS TOSSED OVER THE
LOVESEAT. THE RUG IS A STRIKINGLY BOLD
PATTERN OF TAUPE AND CREAM SISAL
DIAMONDS. BUT NOTHING IS
OVER THE TOP OR TOO SOPHISTICATED.
EVEN THE FLOWERS VORHEES
FAVORS ARE RUSTIC AND PLAIN. A COUPLE
OF FLOWERS PEEK OUT OF THE CORNER
OF A SHELF. ANOTHER VASE
HOLDS STARK, THICK BAYBERRY BRANCHES.

**ABOVE** OUTDOOR SHOWERS ARE ONE
OF THE SYBARITIC MOMENTS
OF SUMMER. THE SHOWER
STALL IS PRIMITIVE
BUT WORTH THE EXPERIENCE.
SHE HAS EQUIPPED HER
SIMPLE HOSE SHOWER WITH BASIC
AMENITIES, SHAMPOO IN A
WHITE MUG, A BAR OF SOAP,
AND AN ENORMOUS THICK
WHITE TOWEL.

**LEFT** THE LADDER LEADS
TO THE SLEEPING LOFT.
"IT'S LIKE A SHIP'S LADDER,"
SAYS VOORHEES.
IT HAS A RIGID WOOD RAILING ON
ONE SIDE AND A ROPE
HANDLE ON THE OTHER.
A SLATTED FOLDING CHILD'S CHAIR
IS ANOTHER OF VOORHEES'S
PERSONAL MEMENTOES.
"IT'S ONE OF THE THINGS I'VE
HAD ALL MY LIFE THAT I LIKE TO KEEP,"
SHE SAYS. A MYRTLE TOPIARY
ADDS SHAPE, COLOR, AND TEXTURE
TO THE SPACE.

**BELOW AND OPPOSITE** NANTUCKET
IS THE KIND OF PLACE
WHERE EVERYONE FLIES AN
AMERICAN FLAG
ON THE FOURTH OF JULY.
VOORHEES'S IS A 48-STAR FLAG
THAT DATES FROM THE 1940S.
SHE CHOSE IT FOR ITS HEAVY WOOL
BUNTING. IT HANGS FROM
A BEAM AND SLIGHTLY
SHIELDS THE ENTRANCE TO
THE SLEEPING LOFT.

P eter Wooster designed the interiors of four restaurants owned by Joe Allen, the Manhattan restaurateur, between 1983 and 1986. In 1987, however, he bought a farmhouse in Roxbury, Connecticut, and has become slowly and fervently obsessed with garden design. "The garden is such a learning experience," he says, "Thomas Jefferson once said that he was an old man but a young gardener." Initially, he was daunted by the notion of making a garden from this former nineteenth-century turkey farm and its surrounding fields. "This end of the field had been a vegetable garden, and the caretaker would plough the fields, and tell me to plant things," says Wooster. "It was completely overwhelming to someone who had spent 20 years in New York." The answer was to divide and conquer. He went out with strings and rulers, divided the garden into segments, and put a fence around it, creating a garden of 100 square

# OUTDOOR LIVING

**OPPOSITE** THE WEATHERED WOOD UMBRELLA MARKS THE MIDDLE OF THE GARDEN, AND BENEATH IS AN EXUBERANT AND LUSH GREEN-ON-GREEN TABLEAU OF POTS FILLED WITH BEGONIA LEAVES SET ON A TABLE. AS IDYLLIC AS THIS SPOT IS, WOOSTER DOES NOT SPEND MUCH TIME HERE. "NO GARDENER CAN CONTEMPLATE FOR LONG," HE EXPLAINS. "BUT THERE ARE MOMENTS IN THE SUMMER, WHEN THE WORKLOAD IS LESS, WHEN YOU CAN SIT AND HAVE COCKTAILS IN THE MIDDLE OF THE DAY."

**RIGHT** WOOSTER'S DISTINCTIVE ORANGE TRUCK ALERTS FRIENDS TO WHEN HE IS HOME.

feet. Within the square garden, there are now six large rectangular beds, each marked with a base of shrubs, conifers, and lots of perennials. Throughout, there are more than 1,500 species of plants and each year he and his gardener edit the collection in an endless search for a different, interesting species. There are 34 varieties of day lilies, which come in colors like vermilion, butter yellow, pearly white, and deep to pale pink. He has nine varieties of buddleia, also known as the butterfly bush, because butterflies, especially the monarchs in this garden, are attracted to the nectar. He grows 30 varieties of canna lilies and 18 varieties of clematis. There are flowers he doesn't even keep track of, as well as sunflowers which thrive without any human help.

On the central axis of the garden is a 1920s cast concrete bird bath. Depending on the day, golden finches, bluebirds, robins, morning doves, and hummingbirds alight on the bath to sip the water. "The garden is as much about birds as it is about flowers," says Wooster, "there's so much to pollinate and to eat." Also marking the center of the garden is the weathered gray wooden umbrella surrounded by a scattering of Adirondack chairs to provide shelter from the sun, a place to read, and to peruse a collection of begonias. Nothing in the garden (except, of course, what Nature does) is entirely happenstance.

In the winter, when the work is minimal, the bare rectilinear bones of the garden stand out: the trees, the shrubs, and even the grasses, which stay up for a while. Even then, the garden is an image of peacefulness.

**LEFT TOP** BUTTERFLIES ARE
ATTRACTED TO THE
BUDDLEIA PLANTS BY THE
NECTAR AND THE POLLEN,
LEADING TO THE
PLANT'S INFORMAL NAME
— THE BUTTERFLY PLANT.

**LEFT MIDDLE** WOOSTER FOUND THIS
SMOOTH, EGG-SHAPED ROCK
IN THE BOTTOM OF THE SHEPAUG
RIVER ONE DAY, WHEN
THERE WAS A DROUGHT AND THE RIVER
WAS NOTHING BUT PEBBLES.
IT RESTS ON A FENCE
BY THE ENTRANCE TO THE GARDEN.

**LEFT BOTTOM** THE RUST-COLORED ARROW
IS PART OF A WEATHERVANE,
WHICH HAS FOUND NEW LIFE
AS A TRELLIS FOR
WHITE MOONFLOWERS.

**OPPOSITE** WOOSTER COMMISSIONED
THE IRON ARCH FROM A
LOCAL BLACKSMITH. "I PLANTED 18
DIFFERENT KINDS OF VINES
IN POCKETS AROUND THE PERIMETER
OF THE GARDEN," WOOSTER
EXPLAINS. "THEY GOT SO MATURE,
THEY STARTED TO COVER THE
GATE, SO I HAD SOMEONE MAKE THE
ARCH SO THEY WOULD GO
UP AND OVER THE GATE."
TRUMPET VINES CLIMB EXUBERANTLY
OVER THE ARCH, GOING FROM
RIGHT TO LEFT.
WHEN THE ARCH STANDS NAKED
IN THE WINTER, "IT LOOKS
LIKE THE VINES," SAYS WOOSTER.

**ABOVE** A CROQUET MALLET LEANS
AGAINST A BLUE METAL
CHAIR. (THERE IS THE OCCASIONAL
GAME OF CROQUET ON
THE LAWN.) TO THE LEFT OF THE
CHAIR IS THE ARISTOLOCHIA
VINE, AND BEHIND THAT IS HOSTA.
SINCE 1987, WHEN HE
FIRST BEGAN TO GARDEN, WOOSTER
HAS DEVELOPED
A CALM ACCEPTANCE ABOUT
THE FACT THAT PLANTS DIE. "IN THE
BEGINNING, YOU REGRET THAT
PLANTS DIE," HE SAYS, "AND THEN YOU
REALIZE IT GIVES YOU A
CHANCE TO BUY SOMETHING NEW."
WHEN AN APRIL SNOW BLEW
THROUGH HIS GARDEN, "ALL THE TENDER
THINGS WENT BROWN AND DEAD,"
HE SAYS. "IT'S A TOUGH PLACE.
THE GROWING SEASON IS SHORT, BUT IT'S
A WONDER TO SEE EVERYTHING."

Gregory Cann, a successful Boston-based interior designer, wanted a house in the woods. His partner, Richard Dickinson, a graphic designer, wanted a house by the beach. So when they found this 1940s cottage in Ogunquit, Maine, they managed to satisfy both their wishes. A small house that nestles in a grove of 100-year-old oak, maple, and hickory trees with a wild garden rampant with bittersweet bishop's weed, it is also only a 10-minute ride from the ocean.

It was built as a temporary home for actors playing at the Ogunquit Playhouse, which was part of the Straw Hat summer theater in the 1940s and 1950s, and included Montgomery Clift and Bette Davis. The actors lived either in or around this house, which was built as a prototype of the one-room cottage that followed. It is tiny – the 407-square-footage includes the deck. Living, dining, and kitchen space are all combined.

# A  PERFECT  MATCH

OPPOSITE THE HOUSE WAS BUILT IN 1940 AS PART OF AN ACTORS' SUMMER COLONY, AND IT IS TINY, JUST 407 SQUARE FEET INCLUDING THE DECK. CANN AND DICKINSON PAINTED THE OUTSIDE OF THE BUILDING GREEN SO THAT IT WOULD BLEND IN WITH THE 100-YEAR-OLD OAK, MAPLE AND HICKORY TREES THAT SURROUND IT.

RIGHT CANN LIKES RAINY DAY PROJECTS, REPETITIVE DECORATIVE MOTIFS, AND BITTERSWEET VINES. SO ONE DAY HE COMBINED THESE THREE PASSIONS, AND MADE THE FAN FROM THE VINES.

"When the Arabs want you to do something creative," says Cann, "they say dream on it." And so the two men did. The house was originally blue-gray, but they decided to paint it a forest green color because Cann wanted it to disappear into the wood. Then they decided to embellish the exterior, mostly with bittersweet vines, which are tough yet malleable. Cann designed a sunburst pattern of the vines, which works as a faux fanlight above the front door, and then used the same vines to wrap around a porch table made of old garden stakes, and also to decorate the kitchen cupboards. "I love repetitive embellishment," says Cann. "I like the continuity of things."

The exterior is green, as is the porch and the Adirondack chairs. The interior, however, is white. "I use the white as an intermezzo, like in a meal," says Cann. An all-white interior, including the floor, makes the house appear larger. "It's a clean palette," according to Cann, "white has always been a Puritan color. It's very calming." In typical New England fashion, little of their furniture is new. Cann salvages jaded pieces with a fresh coat of paint – an old bureau is now a creamy yellow color and a nineteenth-century oak and hickory rocking chair is a chocolate color.

The cottage is the epitome of the word cozy. The two men have designed the house to suit their needs and live with the cooperation, harmony, and diplomacy which the tiny space demands. The ship-shape cottage has a Hansel and Gretel quality to it, as if it just popped out of the forest, but there is no wicked witch.

LEFT  THE OMNIPRESENT WHITE PAINT —
CEILING, WALLS, FLOOR — MAKES THE TINY
COTTAGE FEEL BRIGHT, LIGHT, AND
SPACIOUS. "THE LIVING ROOM
WAS ORIGINALLY ALL PINE, SO WE WENT
FROM QUAINT AND CHARMING
AND WRAPPED IT IN WHITE." SAYS CANN.
THE CAREFUL PLACEMENT OF THE
FURNITURE DELINEATES THE FUNCTION OF
EACH PRECIOUS SQUARE FOOT.
CANN BLEACHED THE GREEN AND WHITE
COTTON TICKING THAT UPHOLSTERS
THE SOFA, AND GAVE IT AN INSTANT
IMPRIMATUR OF AGE.
TO MAKE THE LIVING AREA FRIENDLY,
THEY ADDED A ROCKING CHAIR.

LEFT BELOW  CANN USED YELLOW TO
MAKE THE ROOM APPEAR
GOLDEN. HE PAINTED THE BUREAU A
PALE YELLOW, AND HUNG A YELLOW
-AND-WHITE QUILT ON
THE COMFORTABLE HEADBOARD.

OPPOSITE  CANN BOUGHT CABINETS FROM
THE LOCAL LUMBER YARD,
PAINTED THEM WHITE, AND DECORATED
THEM WITH BITTERSWEET VINES.
HE COVERED THE KITCHEN COUNTER WITH
LAMINATE AND TO SAVE SPACE
HE PUT THE KITCHEN ESSENTIALS OUT IN
THE OPEN. THE DISHES HANG IN
RACKS, THE MUGS ON HOOKS. A TRAY
HANGS ON THE LEFTHAND SIDE
OF THE SINK. SINCE THERE IS NO AIR
CONDITIONING, THE COUPLE
USE OLD-FASHIONED FANS, WHILE THE
CHECKERBOARD TABLE
DOES DOUBLE DUTY AS A GAME
BOARD AND AS A PLACE TO STACK CDS.

**ABOVE** THE DINING AREA OF THIS

COMPACT HOUSE TAKES UP

HALF OF THE LIVING/KITCHEN AREA.

ALTHOUGH THE TABLE ONLY SEATS FOUR

PEOPLE, THE OPEN-PLAN

LIVING AREA MEANS THAT PEOPLE CAN

SIT ON THE SOFA AND NEARBY

CHAIRS AND STILL FEEL INCLUDED IN AN

INTIMATE DINNER PARTY.

**RIGHT** THE HOUSE HAS A TIDY RUSTICITY

ABOUT IT AND EVEN THE

FIREWOOD IS CAREFULLY STACKED.

THE WOOD IS TO BE USED

IN THE NEW WOOD-BURNING STOVE

THAT WILL BE INSTALLED THIS SPRING.

**ABOVE** THE HOUSE MAY BE SMALL,
BUT THE OWNERS HAVE
DECORATED IT WITH CARE.
THEY PAINTED THE ADIRONDACK CHAIRS
GREEN SO THAT THE FURNITURE
WOULD FADE INTO THE LANDSCAPE.
CANN MADE THE SMALL
ROUND TABLE FROM OLD BRANCHES
AND WOOD STAKES WITH
BITTERSWEET VINES WRAPPED AROUND
THE LEGS FOR ANOTHER
RAINY DAY PROJECT. THE ONLY OTHER
COLORS ON THE PORCH ARE
PROVIDED BY THE PLANTS
AND FLOWERS, LIKE THE GOLDENROD
AND FAT SUNFLOWERS.

When Howard Kaminsky was growing up in an apartment in Brooklyn, New York, he had a secret wish. "I always wanted to have a tree house," he says. In 1995, Howard and his wife, Susan, asked John Ryman, an artist and builder, to design a tree house for them and he built a shingle-roofed wooden house nestled 20 feet above the ground amid the branches of a 100-year-old maple tree. Kaminsky also has a traditional house, in northwest Connecticut, together with an assortment of barns and 60 acres of gently rolling land where hay and corn are grown. The area is so pristine and manicured that even a treehouse is built to perfection.

Kaminsky was the president and CEO of Warner Books from 1971 to 1984, and his wife, Susan, has been a copy writer at St. Martins Press, fiction editor for a magazine, and an editor at E. P. Dutton. When they

# THE TREEHOUSE

OPPOSITE A GROWN MAN'S TREEHOUSE, AN URBANITE'S NOTION OF RUSTICITY, PERCHES IN A MAPLE TREE MORE THAN 100 YEARS OLD. THE TREE IS AN INTEGRAL PART OF THE STRUCTURE, WITH BRANCHES ACTING AS STRUCTURAL SUPPORTS BOTH INSIDE AND OUTSIDE THE HOUSE.

RIGHT THE BRANCHES CRISSCROSS AND INTERWINE TO MAKE A NATURAL DECORATION, NOT UNLIKE A FANLIGHT. THE HOUSE WAS PAINTED FOREST GREEN SO THAT IT WOULD BLEND INTO THE TREE. FROM ANY DISTANCE, THE HOUSE IS BARELY VISIBLE, EXCEPT IN WINTER WHEN THE TREE IS STRIPPED BARE OF ITS LEAVES.

decided to collaborate on writing novels, it was a natural collusion of talents. The Kaminskys divide the writing labor. He does the scenario, she pitches her ideas. Each writes a chapter, separately, and with each chapter, they critique each other. He writes in the tree house, she in the main house.

The tree house, perched in a maple tree, overlooks fields of corn and hay and the rolling hills of Connecticut. In the summer, when the hay is high, they mow a path through the hay to the tree house and the maple tree's branches form such a huge canopy that the house disappears into the foliage. The whimsical yet solidly built wood house is high above the ground and is reached by a wood staircase that has 13 steps and handrails. Although this sounds precarious, it is actually very easy to climb. Inside, the trunk and branches of the tree have been adapted into structural supports and partial walls for the house. The house has a lived-in feeling, rustic, weathered, and cozy, with plain furnishings – a desk, bookcases, rocking chair, and a cannonball bed, which serves as a sofa. Tortoiseshell bamboo shades cover the windows, which are a mix of old ones found at auctions and flea markets. Opposite the windows, on the wall above the desk, is bark cloth from Hawaii, which echoes, in its brown and beige colors, the tortoiseshell pattern of the bamboo shades. The walls are white, in contrast to the exterior which is painted a dark forest green to blend in with the verdant surroundings. The floor is also painted a dark green, like the outside of the house.

**ABOVE** THE CENTURY-OLD MAPLE
DWARFS AND SHROUDS THE TREEHOUSE,
WHICH IS 20 FEET IN THE AIR.
THE SIMPLICITY OF THE ANTIQUE DOORS
AND WINDOWS MAKES THE
HOUSE EVEN MORE ANONYMOUS.
TO GET THERE, THE KAMINSKYS CLIMB A
WIDE AND STURDY WOOD
STAIRCASE WITH 13 STEPS AND FIRM
HANDRAILS. THE HOUSE HAS
A LITTLE PORCH, SO THE KAMINSKYS CAN
STEP OUTSIDE TO ADMIRE THEIR
VIEW OF ROLLING FIELDS,
SOME PLANTED WITH HAY AND SOME
WITH CORN FOR ANIMALS.

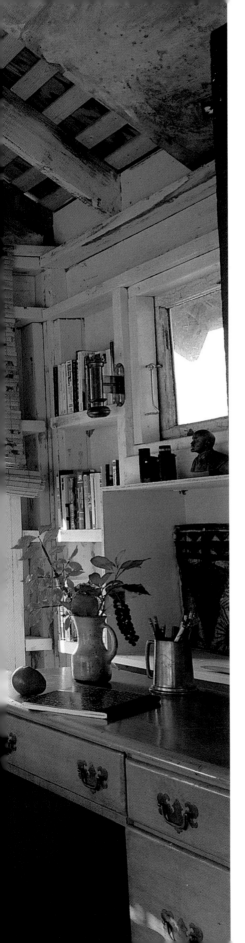

# THE TREEHOUSE

**LEFT** WHEN THE FAMILY IS IN
CONNECTICUT, KAMINSKY HIDES AWAY
IN THE TREEHOUSE AT LEAST ONCE
A DAY, EITHER TO READ OR
TO WRITE. THE FURNISHINGS IN THE
LITTLE HOUSE INCLUDE A
WHITE ROCKING CHAIR, AN OLD DESK
CHAIR AND A CANNONBALL BED.
THE FLOOR IS PAINTED A DARK GREEN,
AND THE WALLS ARE PAINTED
WHITE TO REFLECT
AS MUCH LIGHT AS POSSIBLE.

**RIGHT** PART OF THE TREE
AND ITS CRAGGY BARK BECOMES A
STRUCTURAL WALL, STILL
MANAGING TO LOOK COMPLETELY
NATURAL NEXT TO THE OLD
PAINTED WOOD BOOKCASE AND DOOR
FRAME. THE BOOKCASES
ARE PRIMITIVE BUT FUNCTIONAL.
THROUGHOUT THE TINY HOUSE, THE
DIFFERENT TEXTURES VARY
IN DEGREES OF ROUGHNESS, FROM THE
SMOOTH BAMBOO SHADES
TO THE BARK ON THE TREE.
THE HOUSE IS A WARM, SECURE AND
(ROCK-SOLIDLY BUILT)
CHARMING RETREAT IN WHICH THE
KAMINSKYS CAN DREAM UP
THRILLERS THAT MAY ONE DAY
BECOME MOVIES.

# THE GUIDE

It has often been said that the six states of that make up New England are the most intrinsically American of them all, as well as forming a region steeped in history and tradition. They have much to offer the visitor, from the architectural heritage of the Vanderbilt mansions in Newport, to the shrines to Emily Dickinson and Mark Twain, to the lakes, mountains and ski resorts of Vermont, and the rugged wildness of Maine. The compact size of New England means that it is easy to cover; only rural Maine requires any degree of effort. Though each of the states has a distinct identity, they all offer picturesque towns and dramatic landscapes, especially on the winding coastline. The southern states of Connecticut, Massachusetts, and Rhode Island are more urban, while the northern states are closer to nature.

The following listings are not a comprehensive travel guide, but are meant as a reflection of the ideas and interests of the authors and the inhabitants featured in this book.

# CONNECTICUT

## PLACES TO STAY

*Colony Inn*
1157 Chapel Street
New Haven, CT 06511
tel: 203-776-1234
Colonial-style hotel.

*Lakeview Inn*
107 North Shore Road
New Preston Marble Dale,
CT 06777
tel: 860-868-1000

*Mark Twain Hostel*
131 Tremont Street
Hartford, CT 06105
tel: 860-523-7255
Cheap and comfortable.

*Mayflower Inn & Restaurant*
118 Woodbury Road
Washington, CT 06793
tel: 860-868-9466
Excellent upscale inn, with good
restaurant where California/Asian
meets Continental.

*Residence Inn*
3 Long Wharf Drive
New Haven, CT 06511
tel: 203-777-5337
Luxurious waterfront hotel.

## RESTAURANTS, CAFÉS, AND FOOD STORES

*Atticus Bookstore Café*
1082 Chapel Street
New Haven, CT 06510
tel: 203-776-4040
Coffee and brioche in a friendly
bookstore.

*Brown, Thompson & Co.*
942 Main Street
Hartford, CT 06103
tel: 860-525-1600
Popular downtown restaurant.

*G. W. Tavern*
20 Bee Brook Road
Washington Depot, CT 06794
tel: 860-868-6633
Great American taproom,
serving fish and chips
to filet mignon.

*West Street Grill*
43 West Street
Litchfield, CT 06759
tel: 860-567-1374
American nouvelle cuisine.

## SHOPS

*Gerald Murphy Antiques Limited*
60 Main Street South
Woodbury, CT 06798
tel: 203-266-4211
Seventeenth- to nineteenth-
century antiques.

*J. Seitz*
9 East Shore Road
New Preston Marble Dale,
CT 06777
tel: 860-868-0119
Good range of womenswear
and accessories.

*G. Sergeant Antiques*
88 Main Street North
Woodbury, CT 06798
tel: 203-266-4177

*Michael Trapp*
7 River Road
West Cornwall, CT 06796
tel: 860-672-6098
Sixteenth- to twentieth-century
European, Asian, and African
antiques. Known for garden
and architectural ornaments
and artifacts.

## PLACES TO VISIT

*Housatonic Meadows State Park*
Cornwall Bridge, CT 06754
Picnicking and canoe rides on
the Housatonic River.
Open year-round.

*Macedonia Brook State Park*
159 Macedonia Brook Road
Kent, CT 06757
Waterfalls, great place to picnic
and take short, pleasant,
peaceful walks.

*Mystic Seaport*
Southeast Connecticut
Meticulously constructed
waterfront village at the mouth of
Mystic River.

# MAINE

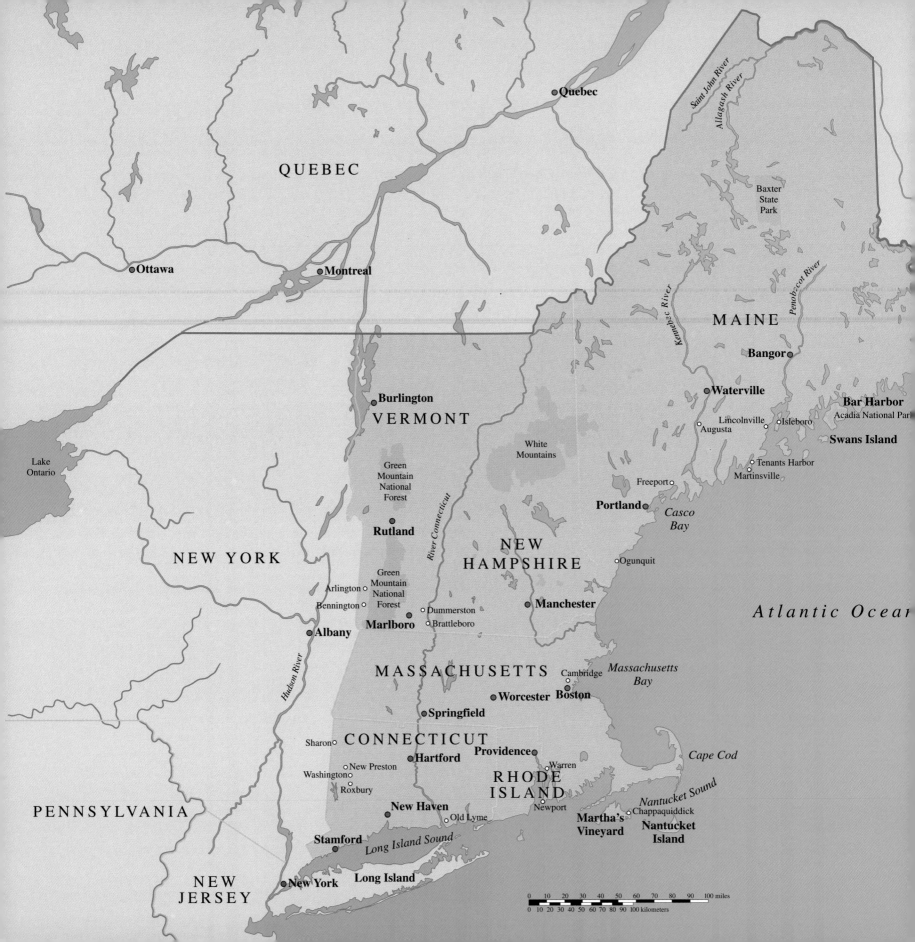

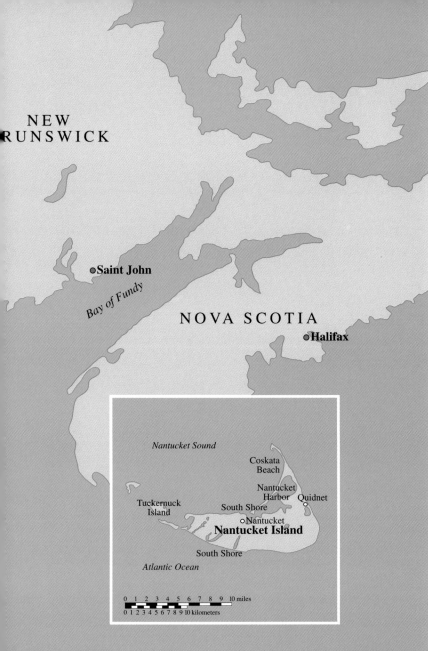

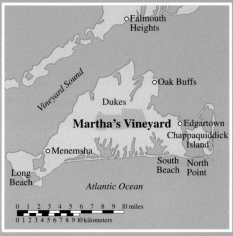

Miranda Café
15 Oak Street
Rockland, ME 04841
tel: 207-594-2034
Good wines.

Moody's Diner
Waldoboro, ME 04572
tel: 207-832-7785
Wooden booths, sassy waitresses
and the best homemade pies in
the world. The real thing.

Pompeo's Brick Oven Pizza
3 Brentwood Street
Portland, ME 03907
tel: 207-774-6844
Good, inexpensive Italian food.

Port Clyde General Store
St. George Street
Port Clyde, ME 04855
tel: 207-372-6543
Sandwiches and picnics to go.

Provisions
650 Main Street
Rockland, ME 04841
tel: 207-594-9063

Second Read Books & Coffee
328 Main Street
Rockland, ME 04841
tel: 207-594-4123

Coffee and tea in a second-hand
bookstore.

Stonewall Kitchen
469 Route 1
York, ME 03909
tel: 207-351-2712
Gourmet preserves, mustards,
and salad dressings.

Thomaston Café & Bakery
88 Main Street
Thomaston, ME 04861
tel: 207-354-8589
A menu of wholesome American
home cooking including
homemade soups, chowders, and
island crabcakes.

BOATING AND YACHTING

The schooner fleets in the
Camden, Rockport, and
Rockland area are known
to the locals as "skinboats"
because of the vacationers
trying to perfect their tans;
they are frequently tied up at
the dock and can be viewed
with their hired crews loafing
or doing maintenance.
Some do day trips but most go
out on one-week excursions.

*American Eagle & Heritage Schooners*
Front Street
Rockland, ME 04841
tel: 207-594-8007
Schooner trips of 3–10 days.

*Brooklin Boatyard*
Center Harbor Road
Brooklin, ME 04616
tel: 207-359-2236
Brooklin is the sanctum sanctorum of wooden boat building in the United States. It was also the home of E. B. White, the children's book writer. White's grandson, Steve, owns and runs the Brooklin Boatyard, where one new boat is always being built.

*Classic Yacht Shantih II*
Rockport Marine Park
Rockport, ME 04856
tel: 207-236-8605
Yacht day cruises.

*Monhegan-Thomaston Boat Line*
Port Clyde, ME 04855
tel: 207-372-8848
Ferry to Monhegan Island, a major attraction for tourists.

*Schooner J & E Riggin*
136 Holmes Street
Rockland, ME 04841
tel: 207-594-1875
Schooner trips of 4–6 days.

*Woodenboat School*
Naskeag Point Road
Brooklin, ME 04616
tel: 207-359-4651
Boatbuilding and sailing courses.

GALLERIES AND MUSEUMS

*The Farnsworth Art Museum*
(the Farnsworth Center for the Wyeth family in Maine)
352 Main Street
Rockland, ME 04841
tel: 207-596-6457
Definitive collection of work by the Wyeth family, widely considered America's most famous family of artists.

*Harbor Square Gallery*
374 Main Street
Rockland, ME 04841
tel: 207-594-8700
or 877-594-8700
Art, jewelry, sculpture, local artists' work. The owner is a renowned goldsmith.

*Islands of Maine Gallery*
412 Main Street
Rockland, ME 04841
tel: 207-596-0701

*Maine Coast Artists*
162 Russell Avenue
Rockport, ME 04856
tel: 207-236-2875
Open Tues–Sat 10 am–5 pm, Sun midday–5 pm. Contemporary work by Maine artists.

*Maine Watercraft Museum*
4 Knox Street Landing
Thomaston, ME 04861
tel: 207-594-0043
email: oldboats@midcoast.com
In-the-water, hands-on display of antique and classic small craft, like Kennebecs, Old Towns, and Skowhegans. Some can be rented by the hour. Boat rides offered, depending on the weather.

*Maine State Museum*
State House Complex
Augusta, ME 04333
tel: 207-287-2301
Augusta is the state capital, and the museum has displays and artifacts of Maine history including exhibits featuring a paper mill and logging operation.

*Owls Head Transportation Museum*
117 Museum Street
Owls Head, ME 04854
tel: 207-594-4418
Meticulously maintained old cars and aircraft.

*Westbrook College Art Gallery*
University of New England
716 Stevens Avenue
Portland, ME 04103
tel: 207-797-7261
Once home to Van Gogh's *Irises*, the gallery has small shows which are just the right size to fit into a spare hour.

SHOPS

*ABCD Books*
23 Bay View Street
Camden, ME 04843
tel: 207-236-3903
www.abcdbooks.com
Bookstore specializing in old and rare books about ships, Maine history, poetry and prose of the nineteenth and twentieth century, and rare children's books.

*Blue Hill Antiques*
8 Water Street
Blue Hill, ME 04614
tel: 207-374-8825
Quilts and eighteenth- and
nineteenth-century French
antiques.

*Swans Island Blankets*
Swans Island, ME 04685
tel: 207-526-4492
www.atlanticblanket.com
John and Carolyn Grace make
fine natural handwoven and
hand-dyed wool blankets.

*Wayway General Store*
93 Buxton Road
Saco, ME 04072
tel: 207-283-1362
The way life used to be, complete
with gas pumps and outhouses as
well as penny candy and beans in
bins to supply the churches for
local bean suppers.

PLACES OF INTEREST

*Acadia National Park*
Eagle Lake Road
Mount Desert, ME
tel: 207-288-3338
Friends of Acadia
tel: 207-288-3340
Beautiful hiking trails with views
of the ocean. People walk or ride
bicycles or horses on more than
100 miles of carriage trails built
by the Rockefeller family. The
trails are closed to traffic.

*Bryant's Stove Works*
Thorndike, ME 04986
tel: 207-568-3665
Splendid collection of restored
antique wood stoves, player
pianos, and calliopes for sale.

*Bradbury Mountain State Park*
Pownal, Maine, about 20 miles
north of Portland on Route 9
Mini-hikes on a mini-mountain
that won't wear you out. A
favorite for class picnics.

*The village of Castine, ME*
near Bangor, ME
A seaside New England town for
the very well off that has not
changed for centuries except for
the powerlines and paved roads.

*Kelmscott Farm*
Lincolnville, ME 04849
tel: 207-763-4088
For animal-loving children, a
place where endangered breeds of
sheep and horses are raised.
Weavers and spinners can buy
raw fleece by the pound,
from Cotswold, Jacob, and
Shetland sheep.

*Penobscot Marine Museum*
Church Street
Searsport, ME 04974
tel: 207-548-2529
In the nineteenth century,
Searsport was home to many of
America's sea-going captains.
Some of the original sea captains'
homes are still intact. The
museum has a collection of
marine paintings, and small craft
and ship models.

*Popham Beach*
Route 209, 14 miles from Bath
toward Phippsburg
Mainers come here for the
shifting tidal pools, sand dunes,
and dramatic currents.

*Rachel Carson National
Wildlife Refuge*
Wells, ME 04090
tel: 207-646-9226
The refuge will eventually
encompass 7,435 acres. Now,
more than 250 species of birds
including Canada geese, black
ducks, and green-winged teal
thrive. Early settlers
found the marshland valuable
as a source for salt marsh hay.

# MASSACHUSETTS

**Martha's Vineyard**

PLACES TO STAY

*Charlotte Inn*
South Summer Street
Edgartown, MA 02539
tel: 508-627-4751
Every room furnished with
antiques. Great restaurant.

*Martha's Place*
114 Main Street
Vineyard Haven, MA 02568
tel: 508-693-0253

*Outermost Inn*
Lighthouse Road
Gay Head, MA 02535
tel: 508-645-3511
email:
inquiries@outermostinn.com
Hugh Taylor, a brother of the
singer, James Taylor, is one
of the owners of this inn.

RESTAURANTS, CAFÉS, AND
FOOD STORES

*Alchemy*
71 Main Street
Edgartown, MA 02539
tel: 508-627-9999
Bistro.

*Balance*
57 Circuit Avenue
Oak Bluffs, MA 02557
tel: 508-696-3000

*Cafe Moxie*
48 Main Street
Vineyard Haven, MA 02568
tel: 508-693-1484
Locals eat here. Bring your
own wine.

*Lola's*
Beach Road
Oak Bluffs, MA 02557
tel: 508-693-5007
Good, hearty Southern and
Cajun food. Live music, mostly
blues and jazz.

SHOPS

*Bramhall & Dunn*
Main Street
Vineyard Haven, MA 02568
tel: 508-693-6437
Garden ornaments and
hand-knit sweaters.

*Chicamoo*
Lamberts Cove Road
West Tisbury, MA 02575
tel: 508-693-6291

Richard Lee is a partner
in this store and art gallery,
which sells local nineteenth-
century antiques, all
refurbished and often
painted with faux finishes.

*Claudia*
51 Main Street
Edgartown, MA 02539
tel: 508-627-8306
*and* 64 Main Street
Vineyard Haven, MA 02568
tel: 508-693-5465
New eclectic jewelry,
including Claudia Lee's
delicate pieces made from
semi-precious stones.

*Country Life*
Main Street
Vineyard Haven, MA 02568
tel: 508-693-2243
New and vintage decorative
accessories and home
furnishings.

*Craven Gallery*
495A State Road
West Tisbury, MA 02575
tel: 508-693-3535

*Field Gallery and Sculpture
Garden*
State Road
West Tisbury, MA 02575
tel: 508-693-5595
Kinetic sculpture, Jules Feiffer
cartoons.

*Hermine Merel Smith Fine Art*
548 Edgartown Road
West Tisbury, MA 02575
tel: 508-693-7719
Paintings.

*Granary Gallery*
Old County Road
West Tisbury, MA 02575
tel: 508-693-0455
Island-oriented art, including
landscape paintings and
photography, and antique
painted furniture.

*Past and Presents*
37 and 42 Main Street
Edgartown, MA 02539
tel: 508-627-6686/ 508-627-3992
British and American antique
furniture and work by
local artists.

PLACES OF INTEREST

*The Lighthouse at Gay Head*
A town now being called by
its original Native American
name, Aquinnah, Gay Head
is famous for its cliffs, which
overlook the ocean and the
Elizabeth Islands.

*The Edgartown Lighthouse*
Edgartown, MA

*Whaling captains' homes*
Edgartown, MA

*The island of Chappaquiddick*
Take the On-Time ferry from
Edgartown. A car or bicycle
is necessary to get around
the island, which is famous
for its beauty.

*Campgrounds*
Oak Bluffs, MA
A community of gingerbread
cottages built in the Twenties
and Thirties from kits.
One is called the Valentine
House and is painted bright
red and pink.

**Nantucket**
PLACES TO STAY

*The House of Orange*
25 Orange Street
Nantucket, MA 02554
tel: 508-228-9287

*Quaker House*
5 Chestnut Street
Nantucket, MA 02554
tel: 508-228-0400

*Pineapple Inn*
10 Hussey Street
Nantucket, MA 02554
tel: 508-228-9992

RESTAURANTS, CAFÉS, AND
FOOD STORES

*Straight Wharf Restaurant*
Straight Wharf
Nantucket, MA 02554
tel: 508-228-4499

*21 Federal Restaurant*
21 Federal Street
Nantucket, MA 02554
tel: 508-228-2121

*Le Languedoc Inn & Restaurant*
24 Broad Street
Nantucket, MA 02554
tel: 508-228-2552

*Kendrick's at the Quaker House*
5 Chestnut Street
Nantucket, MA 02554
tel: 508-228-9156

SHOPS

*Flowers on Chestnut*
1 Chestnut Street
Nantucket, MA 02554
tel: 508-228-6007

*Margareta Nettles Weaving
Studio*
64 Union Street
Nantucket, MA 02554
tel: 508-228-9533
Custom-made woven Swedish
wool double-sided tapestry rugs.

*Nantucket Country*
38 Center Street
Nantucket, MA 02554
tel: 508-228-8868
Antiques shop owned by Cam
and Gardiner Dutton specializing
in eighteenth- and nineteenth-
century Americana.

*Nantucket Looms*
16 Main Street
Nantucket, MA 02554
tel: 508-228-1908
Beautifully woven blankets,
spreads, and throws.

*Weeds*
14 Center Street
Nantucket, MA 02554
tel: 508-228-5200
Nineteenth-century French and
English antiques. Owned by Geo.
Davis.

PLACES OF INTEREST

*Nantucket Historical Association*
2 Whalers Lane
Nantucket, MA 02554
tel: 508-228-1894
The Nantucket Historical
Association runs many
of the historical sites on the
island, including the Whaling
Museum on Broad Street,
which documents the great
whaling era of Nantucket,
and the Oldest House on
Sunset Hill.

# NEW HAMPSHIRE

### PLACES TO STAY

*A Touch of Europe*
85 Centre Street
Concord, NH 03301
tel: 603-226-3771
Victorian-style lodgings.

*Bow Street Inn*
121 Bow Street
Portsmouth, NH 03801
tel: 603-431-7760
The only waterfront inn in
Portsmouth.

*The Inn at Christian Shores*
335 Maplewood Avenue
Portsmouth, NH 03801
tel: 603-431-6770
Nineteenth-century Federal
house.

*The Inn at Strawberry Banke*
314 Court Street
Portsmouth, NH 03801
tel: 603-436-7242
Sumptuous old colonial home.

*Martin Hill Inn*
404 Islington Street
Portsmouth, NH 03801
tel: 603-436-2287
Nineteenth-century house.

### RESTAURANTS, CAFÉS, AND FOOD STORES

*BG's Boat House Restaurant*
191 Wentworth Road
Portsmouth, NH 03801
tel: 603-431-1074
Clam rolls, lobster rolls,
and oyster rolls, with views
of the water.

*Celebrity Sandwich*
171 Islington Street
Portsmouth, NH 03801
tel: 603-433-2277
Enormous deli sandwiches.

*Karen's Restaurant*
637 Daniel Street
Portsmouth, NH 03801
tel: 603-431-1948
Creative American
nouvelle cuisine.

*The Stockpot*
53 Bow Street
Portsmouth, NH 03801
tel: 603-431-1851
Reasonably priced hearty
American food.

### BOATING AND YACHTING

*Buccaneer Charters*
177 Mechanic Street
Portsmouth, NH 03801
tel. 603-431-6999
Evening cruises, harbor tours,
and trips to the Isles of Shoals.

*Isles of Shoals Steamship
Company*
315 Market Street
Portsmouth, NH 03801
tel: 603-431-5500
Cruises and whale watches.

*MS Mount Washington*
Lake Winnipesaukee, NH
tel: 603-366-5531
Scenic day and dinner cruises.

### GALLERIES AND MUSEUMS

*Currier Gallery of Art*
201 Myrtle Way
Manchester, NH 03104
tel: 603-626-4158
New Hampshire's best fine arts
museum. Also maintains the
Zimmerman House, a one-story
wooden building designed by
Frank Lloyd Wright.

*Strawberry Banke Museum*
454 Court Street
Portsmouth, NH 03801
tel: 603-433-1100
Nine furnished houses and
period gardens on the 10-acre
site recreate over 300 years
of life in the Puddle Dock
neighborhood.

### PLACES TO VISIT

*Portsmouth Harbor Trail*
Portsmouth, NH 03801
tel: 603-436-1118
Fascinating walking tours
following the history of
this town.

*State House*
Main Street
Concord, NH 03301
tel: 603-271-2154
Golden-domed state building.

# RHODE ISLAND

*Cliffside Inn*
2 Seaview Avenue
Newport, RI 02840
tel: 401-847-1811
Victorian manor house.

*Old Court*
144 Benefit Street
Providence, RI 02903
tel: 401-751-2002
A nineteenth-century brick
rectory turned bed and breakfast.

*Jailhouse Inn*
13 Marlborough Street
Newport, RI 02840
tel: 401-847-4638
Restored 1772 jailhouse building.

*Providence Biltmore*
Kennedy Plaza
Providence, RI 02903
tel: 401-421-0700
The old-time hotel, where
parents of Brown and RISD
students inevitably stayed when
they dropped their children
off for school, was renovated in
1996. Once genteel and dowdy,
now it is airy and polished.

*Providence Marriott*
1 Orms Street
Providence, RI 02906
tel: 401-272-2400
A family-friendly hotel.
There's an indoor-outdoor
pool, and a disco.

*Westin Providence*
1 West Exchange Street
Providence, RI 02502
tel: 401-598-8000
The 25-floor post-modern
building was built in 1994, and
has an airy two-story rotunda
lobby, a health spa, and
a seafood restaurant
called Agora.

RESTAURANTS, CAFÉS, AND
FOOD STORES

*Al Forno*
577 Main Street South,
Providence, RI 02903
tel: 401-273-9760
Famous for grilling meats over
wood fires; the herbed chicken,
duck and steak are all super.
Equally famous are the incredibly
thin pizzas.

*Aunt Carrie's Restaurant*
1240 Ocean Road
Narragansett, RI 02882
tel: 401-783-7930
Classic delectable shore dinner:
chowder, steamer clams, deep-
fried clam fritters, corn on the
cob, and lobster.

*The Black Pearl*
Bannister's Wharf
Newport, RI 02840
tel: 401-846-5264
Newport institution renowned for
its chunky clam chowder.

*Bouchard Restaurant*
505 Thames Street
Newport, RI 02840
tel: 401-846-0123
Elegant French food.

*CAV Restaurant, Antiques
and Gifts*
14 Imperial Place
Providence, RI 02903
tel: 401-751-9164
Fashionable restaurant in
historical loft.

*Coffee Exchange*
207 Wickenden Street
Providence, RI 02903
tel: 401-273-1198
Trendy coffee bar where deck
chairs and barrels act as
pavement seating.

*The Cooke House*
Bannisters Wharf
Newport, RI 02840
tel: 401-849-2900
The restaurant has several floors,
each one different. There's
elegant dining on one floor, a
small bar and a simpler menu on
another, and dancing on a third.

*The Place at Yesterday's*
28 Washington Square
Newport, RI 02840
tel: 401-847-0125
"Everybody in Newport eats
here," says Ainslie Gardner.

*White Horse Tavern*
Marlborough
Newport, RI 02840
tel: 401-849-3600
Excellent food in an
eighteenth-century house.

SHOPS

*Brick Market*
off Long Wharf, downtown
Newport, RI 02840
Market dating from 1762 also
includes galleries and shops.

*Richard Kazarian Antiques*
325 Water Street
Warren, RI 02885
tel: 401-245-0700
American, European,
architectural, and
garden antiques.

GALLERIES AND MUSEUMS

*Coggeshall Farm Museum*
Colt State Park
Bristol, RI 02809
tel: 401-253-9062
A 35-acre outdoor museum
representing a Rhode Island
coastal farm in the 1790s.

*Haffenreffer Museum of
Anthropology*
Mount Hope Grant
Bristol, RI 02809
tel: 401-253-1287
Thousands of artifacts from
Africa, Asia, and Latin America.

*Museum of Art, Rhode Island
School of Design*
College Street
Providence, RI 02902
tel: 401-454-6500
This small but exquisite museum
has the largest wooden Buddha
outside Japan, four Copleys,
some excellent Impressionists,
and two paintings by the Cuban
artist Wilfredo Lam.

PLACES OF INTEREST

*Blithewold Mansion and
Gardens*
101 Ferry Road
Bristol, RI 02809
tel: 401-253-2707
33 acres of landscaped gardens
overlooking Narragansett Bay.
Exotic plants include a bamboo
grove, a 90-foot giant sequoia
tree, and woodland paths.

*Providence Riverwalk*
Providence, RI
The Woonasquatucket,
Moshassuck and Providence
Rivers, which had been paved
over, have now been uncovered,
redirected and landscaped.
On some Saturday evenings,
local artists build 40 bonfires in
braziers, which blaze from dusk
to midnight.

*Preservation Society of Newport
County*
424 Bellevue Avenue
Newport, RI 02840
tel: 401-847-1000
Information and combined
admission tickets to the famous
Newport mansions.

*Quaker Meeting House*
corner of Farewell Street and
Marlborough Street, Newport, RI
tel: 401-846-0813
Free tours of the oldest religious
building (1699) in Newport. By
appointment only.

# VERMONT

## PLACES TO STAY

*3 Church Street*
3 Church Street
Woodstock, VT 05091
tel: 802-457-1925
Pet-friendly Georgian mansion.

*The Artist's Loft B&B and Gallery*
103 Main Street
Brattleboro, VT 05301
tel: 802-257-5181
Luxurious suite above art gallery.

*Four Columns Inn*
21 West Street
Newfane, VT 05345
tel: 802-365-7713
Wonderful inn. Good food.

*The Old Tavern at Grafton*
Grafton, VT 05146
802-843-2231
www.old-tavern.com
Beautiful inn, jazz, good food, big fireplaces.

*Radisson*
60 Battery Street
Burlington, VT 05401
tel: 802-658-6500
Extravagant hotel on a hillside.

## RESTAURANTS, CAFÉS, AND FOOD STORES

*Max's*
414 Western Avenue
Brattleboro, VT 05301
tel: 802-254-7747
Open kitchen. Great food and wine.

*Pane Salut*
61 Central Street
Woodstock, VT 05091
tel: 802-457-4882
Woodstock's best cappuccino.

*Peter Haven's Restaurant*
32 Elliot Street
Brattleboro, VT 05301
tel: 802-257-3333
Upscale, crowded diner.

*Riverview Restaurant*
3 Bridge Street
Brattleboro, VT 05301
tel: 802-254-9841
Tasty, cheap seafood.

*Smoke Jack's*
156 Church Street
Burlington, VT 05401
tel: 802-658-1119
Innovative American cuisine.

*Townshend Dam Diner*
Townshend, VT 05353
tel: 802-874-4107
Breakfast.

## GALLERIES AND MUSEUMS

*The Shelburne Museum*
5555 Shelburne Road
Shelburne, VT 05482
tel: 802-985-3344
Fabulous 50-acre collection of Americana comprised of over 30 buildings, including seven fully furnished historic houses.

*The Vermont Historical Society Museum*
109 State Street
Montpelier, VT 05609
tel: 802-828-2991
Offers a fascinating insight into the state's past.

*Woodstock Folk Art Prints and Antiquities*
6 Elm Street
Woodstock, VT 05091
tel: 802-457-2012
Local folk art and prints.

## SHOPS

*British Clockmaker*
West Street
Newfane, VT 05345
tel: 802-365-7770
Old clocks repaired.

*Sam's Department Stores*
74 Main Street
Brattleboro, VT 05301
tel: 802-254-2933
Wool socks, sporting goods, popcorn machines.

## PLACES OF INTEREST

*Brown & Roberts*
182 Main Street
Brattleboro, VT 05301
tel: 802-257-4566
Old-fashioned hardware store.

# INDEX

## ACKNOWLEDGMENTS

The authors would like to thank all those who have
welcomed them into their homes and opened up
their lives and thoughts, spending time to discuss
the details of their homes.

My thanks go to Trudy Taylor whom I met on
Martha's Vineyard in the early Nineties. Her wisdom
made New England stand out for me as a significant
and fascinating region.

Thanks also to Francine Gardner, Stephen Mack,
and Dennis Kyte whom I met on my research
trip in 1998. It was they (and their homes) who
confirmed my own feeling that I should go ahead
with this project.

Also, to my inner circle – my mother, my
daughter, Camila, and my two dogs – as always,
they have been a source of comfort and are infinitely
precious to me.

SØLVI DOS SANTOS

I would like to thank James Grossman, Joelle
Madiec, Anne Zill and Robert and Marjory Potts for
their hospitality and for explaining the subtleties of
life in Maine and Martha's Vineyard. Finally, thanks
to Robert Grossman, Tracy Turner, and Anna
Sussman for their sweet support.

ELAINE LOUIE

Simon & Schuster
Rockefeller Center
1230 Avenue of the Americas
New York, NY 10020

Photographs © Sølvi dos Santos 2000
Text © Elaine Louie 2000
Design and layout © Conran Octopus Limited 2000
Map illustration © Conran Octopus Limited 2000

Art editor: Karen Bowen
Map illustrator: Russell Bell
Production: Sarah Tucker/Alex Wiltshire

Published by arrangement with Conran Octopus
Limited

SIMON & SCHUSTER and colophon are registered
trademarks of Simon & Schuster, Inc.

Manufactured in China

10 9 8 7 6 5 4 3 2 1

Library of Congress Cataloguing-in-Publication
Data is available.

ISBN 0-7432-0375-5